Asking For a Friend

Answers from the Universe to Life's Big Questions

HELEN JACOBS

PSYCHIC

murdoch books

Sydney | London

A trained journalist, Helen Jacobs was a successful PR and marketing executive who left her thriving career to become a full-time psychic, hosting popular workshops and events to provide thousands of readings for people all over the world. In addition to her work as a medium, Helen mentors and teaches women how to change their lives and find a more meaningful path for themselves. Her first book, *You Already Know: How to access your intuition and find your divine life path,* is also published by Murdoch Books.

Published in 2021 by Murdoch Books, an imprint of Allen & Unwin

Murdoch Books Australia
83 Alexander Street, Crows Nest NSW 2065
Phone: +61 (0)2 8425 0100
murdochbooks.com.au
info@murdochbooks.com.au

Murdoch Books UK
Ormond House, 26–27 Boswell Street, London WC1N 3JZ
Phone: +44 (0) 20 8785 5995
murdochbooks.co.uk
info@murdochbooks.co.uk

A catalogue record for this book is available from the National Library of Australia

A catalogue record for this book is available from the British Library

ISBN 978 1 92235 143 2 Australia
ISBN 978 1 91166 820 6 UK

Cover and text design by Emily O'Neill
Typeset by Midland Typesetters, Australia
Printed and bound in Australia by Griffin Press

10 9 8 7 6 5 4 3 2 1

The paper in this book is FSC® certified. FSC® promotes environmentally responsible, socially beneficial and economically viable management of the world's forests.

Contents

For all those asking the big questions.

Introduction

Imagine you were about to get your one big, burning life question answered – what would you ask? Would you ask a question you hadn't ever wanted to be seen asking, a question you thought might inadvertently reveal your true feelings or desires? Or perhaps there's some part of your life you've always wanted to understand, to contextualise and illuminate why you are the way you are – that might be your question. Many of us are asking important questions about the state of our planet and its people, and the very future of our world. Regardless of the kind of question, no doubt there's at least one percolating in your mind right now that you would love an answer to. So, really think about it: if you had the chance to ask your question, what would you ask? And, perhaps more importantly, would you be truly willing to receive the answer?

No matter our differences, we all ultimately ask the same big life questions. When will I find love? What happens when we die? Why do bad things happen to good people? Why did this happen to me? While there may not be a definitive answer to such questions, the current climate of our world certainly creates the perfect reason to now ask and explore such questions.

I've asked my fair share of big, burning life questions. These questions – and their answers – led me to asking thousands and thousands more. Not all these questions were for me; I've been busy asking for friends. And, no, I don't have thousands and thousands of friends (I'm actually an introvert). I'm more of a medium, literally asking for a friend. For the past thirteen years, I've relayed myriad questions from my clients to the realm of spirit, using my abilities as a psychic, channel and spiritual medium (more on that in a moment) to help my clients answer their own big, burning questions. Over this time, I've pretty much been asked everything – and been equally surprised by many of the answers spirit served up, too.

I've had clients ask me all kinds of things – from the mundane questions regarding misplaced items through to whether they can engage in sex with a spirit (turns out, sexual energy can indeed be exchanged, but the physicality is rather difficult when one party lacks a body). Quickly enough, I concluded that these weren't the kinds of questions and answers I enjoyed relaying.

It also didn't take me long to observe that everyone who came through my doors thought they were the only person asking me their one burning question. They weren't. I essentially relayed the same messages (albeit with tweaks pertinent for the client before me) over and over again.

Sometimes I can be asked the essence of the same question by two different people and I'll answer it completely differently. Such answers aren't merely a formulaic response. Rather, when I seek answers for someone, a lot goes on behind the scenes. Spirit looks at the big picture of someone's life – their current energetic set point, their current belief system and world view, their levels of self-love and what they believe is possible for them. Spirit is more interested in what that particular individual's soul path is – so, Person A may need to take the job, make the change or take the step because it's where *they* need to learn, while Person B is advised against it. It's not for them, and it's not where they need to go to learn.

With that in mind, as you read these questions and answers, you might see yourself reflected in them. No matter how closely someone's story or situation may resemble your own, please don't automatically assume the answers are right for you. Trust your own intuition and judgement for that (or work with someone who can tune into *your* path and purpose). Instead, notice what stands out for you, what jars you or even what advice *you* may want to offer – these are all clues to the information you need to hear right now. Because such questions and answers are likely to produce even more personal questions for you, I've included a 'Questions to Ask Yourself' section at the close of each chapter. And, because I truly believe such questions will prompt an even deeper self-guided exploration (and I want you to remember your own powerful intuition), I've also bundled up the best tips, tools and resources I couldn't fit into this book into a free downloadable resource on my website. You'll find it at helenjacobs. co/ask, along with The Little Sage Oracle Cards, mentioned in the 'Questions to Ask Yourself' sections and channelled through me from spirit.

Because there is no one-size-fits-all answer to life's big questions, my personal mission has deepened from those early days as a psychic reader into more of a teacher and mentor. **I believe it's more important to help people understand *how* to answer questions for themselves than to keep answering their questions for them.** When the nature of our personal questions changes, *and our approach to answering them changes too*, we begin a much deeper process of self-discovery. If we shift our perception of such questions (and their answers) from a purely intellectual lens to one of spiritual growth, our curiosity can actually help align us with our own divine life path.

So why, then, write a book relaying all the curly questions and answers?

Great question, friend.

One reason for this book is a last hoorah of sorts for me. After answering thousands of questions for well over a decade, I've observed a shift. People are increasingly ready to take back their power and reclaim their own inherent intuitive gifts to remember who they are and why they're here. Gone are the days psychics were consulted for entertainment, or inadvertently handed someone's personal power as they falsely deemed the psychic 'all-knowing'. Instead, everyday people are remembering they, too, were born with tremendous intuitive gifts – and now want to learn how to put them to use. My role is to help guide them and teach them *how*. As such, my teaching and mentoring role needs more of my attention. I trust this book will provide a little psychic FAQ for those fleeting moments when you feel you may still need outside counsel.

The main reason for this book, however, arose out of a query I (rather ironically) asked of spirit, questioning whether or not I should even write this book. Their answer suggested I probably should.

Let me explain.

Early in 2020, I met with my publisher at Murdoch Books, Kelly Doust. My first title, *You Already Know*, had been out a few months and so Kelly enquired if I had any new book ideas. I did not. Kelly proposed to me the idea for this very book you're now reading – and my first response was uncertainty. Was I ready to tackle the mammoth task of writing another book so soon? Was it really the time for a book such as this? And was it for me to write?

As I left that meeting, I asked spirit for a sign. Making my way through peak-hour traffic in the rain, I pulled up at a set of traffic lights. Noticing the bright orange car pulling up in the lane beside me, I then noticed its numberplate. If you've read *You Already Know*, you know I'm a sucker for a message via a numberplate. Lo and behold, this personalised numberplate read WRI73, which, when read interpreting the 73 as a T and an E, looks more like WRITE.

Thus, I got the sign – and answer to my own burning question – that this book was indeed needed.

But, I still wasn't ready.

Just a few weeks later, our world began to shut down as the COVID-19 pandemic swept across the globe. While holed up at home, juggling business and homeschooling like the rest of the world, I had another conversation with Kelly. I finally caught up with what Kelly and my spirit guides had known all along – this was most definitely the time for a book such as this.

As our world rapidly and radically changed before us, people were suddenly asking bigger questions than ever before, not only of me, but of themselves and others. And suddenly the spirit world had a lot more to say, too.

Now may be a good time, especially if you're new to me and my work, to share how I closely work with a group of spirit guides (non-physical guiding beings) whom I call my Spiritual Support Team, or SST. These are a group of higher vibrational beings, individually and collectively assigned to working with us for our spiritual growth and development. Yes, you have them, too. Each guide plays a specific role as they counsel you along your life path. You'll hear me affectionately refer to my SST simply as Chris. Why, you ask? Very early on in my relationship with my SST, my now-husband Gary affectionately called them Chris in an attempt to avoid awkward conversations in coffee shops being overheard by nearby ears. And so, Chris stuck.

I didn't always know I was communicating with the world of spirit, however. In 2001, my aunt passed away and subsequently visited me in spirit, over the course of several hours, with my family as witness, just a few weeks following her death. With that forever life-altering morning, I was thrust into the realisation I could indeed communicate with the world of spirit. I share the story in more detail in *You Already Know*. Suffice to say here that her visitation was the catalyst for quite the spiritual awakening, eventually culminating in me leaving my public relations career to begin giving psychic readings. Since then, I've been privileged to grow and lead a thriving online community of everyday people living more intuitively.

It wasn't long before another group of guiding beings, who call themselves the High Council of Sages, joined with my SST.

They are a group of beings assigned to work with the masses of people awakening on our planet – and so, while such a mass spiritual awakening was occurring during the COVID-19 pandemic, they had a lot to say. As a psychic and channel, I bring through their messages for my clients and community.

Chris and the Council (sounds like some kind of cosmic boy band, huh?) have been sharing a lot about the direction our world is heading in. This higher level guidance is shared via my podcast, *The Guided Collective*, as well as to members of my online communities. In my free 2020 Annual Collective Energy Forecast (it's still available on the podcast) and via my weekly forecasts and predictions, spirit foretold the timings of such change and our questioning of the meaning of it all.

Perhaps not surprisingly, my inbox was flooded and attendance at my monthly online events skyrocketed. People wanted answers. We don't just want to know about our love lives and careers anymore (although, we really still do). Instead, we suddenly escalated our questions to our place – and survival – in the world.

I believe our pivot point is here. Such a wake-up call is awakening the masses to their spirituality and their soul – and to asking bigger questions than ever before. As the trajectory of our humanity and the planet itself veers off-course, we must look beyond our individual ego-centric desires if we're to benefit the whole. Our collective crisis point is our moment of collective awakening. Asking the right questions, and allowing a higher perspective in the answers, can help us turn this around. My hope is that a book such as this, dealing with those big questions, can reach more people than I will ever be able to on my own at a time when it's so very needed.

Asking for a Friend shares a collection of questions and answers from the past decade. For privacy, identifying features and details have been changed and some questions have been combined, but the essence remains. What you find here are the answers I received from Chris, and sometimes the Council, shared with my words and interpretations.

My wish for you as you encounter these questions and answers is a greater sense of hope and possibility. Even in our darkest moments, we are never truly alone and things are never quite as bad as they seem. When we can gain a new (mostly higher) perspective we tend to rise above the minutiae of our life's problems, and feel like we can – *and will* – make change. That's not to minimise our situation, of course. Many of life's hardships are indeed hard, painful, raw and traumatic. This book is no substitute for healing; there's no bypassing the deep work here. Instead, this book serves as a gentle reminder to lean into another meaning and to perhaps entertain another potential outcome so full of wild possibility your mind cannot yet fathom it for itself.

As I write this introduction, I'm watching the sunrise over the ocean at a beach aptly named Sunrise Beach. Waves keep rolling in. Clouds keep blowing through. And the sun's light rises to greet us once more. No matter the season you are in, no matter the questions swirling around your mind right now, the waves will subside, the clouds will blow through and light will return again. Your own light never stops shining. Perhaps, like the sun, it's just been out of view.

While you're waiting for your own light to illuminate answers to your own big questions, may this book and the myriad questions I've asked for friends shed light for you in the meantime.

Choose your adventure

Many a question has resulted from a proverbial fork in the road. This way, or that? Such choices and decisions prompt us to seek confirmation or external advice and, while I am dedicated to helping people remember their own answers, there are always going to be times we seek outside counsel. Please, though, don't forget you are a powerful being with your own internal navigation system and a higher source of guidance in the world of spirit. Alas, we're also human – which means we have a tendency to forget our own power and seek to ask others for their input, right?

Maybe you, too, have asked yourself:

- Am I making the right choice?

- What if I get it wrong?

- Will I miss out on something so much better – or just miss out altogether?

No matter the options before us, such choices tend to present some sort of internal conflict as we consider the alternatives. We project multiple potential scenarios. We weigh pros and cons. We even try to anticipate – or manipulate – the outcomes. Spirit sees these choices and outcomes differently than our human minds do. Spirit's perspective focuses on our life path, soul growth and lessons more than our ego's focus on desired outcomes. Our specific options and choices will be as varied as the people reading this book. Nonetheless, the questions and answers here offer a cross-section of the ways we can face and navigate our own forks in the road, and illuminate the alternative perspective spirit sheds on the decision-making process.

Decision paralysis

Q *I have a history of procrastination. Maybe I'm just lazy. I actually don't know how to make a decision, especially big decisions. I feel like everyone else has some special ability to know how to do the right thing – was there some life-skill lesson taught at school that I was absent for? How am I meant to make decisions, especially hard decisions, without becoming paralysed or messing it up?*

A We can be so hard on ourselves, can't we? Labelling yourself as lazy isn't going to help you make decisions; if anything it will only demotivate you further. Perhaps calling yourself lazy is your mind trying to keep you stuck in such a self-fulfilling prophecy. You are a wondrously capable human being who is perhaps just a little scared (your procrastination gave it away). And fear is a lot easier to work through when you know how.

Here's a useful process not necessarily to make decisions, but to remind yourself you are wildly capable of doing so.

1. Identify what you're worried about

Maybe try a pros and cons list. Talk it out or write it down. However you want to do it, just get the thoughts and beliefs out of your head – it's a lot easier to fix something when you've identified what it is you're dealing with.

2. Where did this worry originate?

Knowing what you're scared of makes it easier to work through that fear. Maybe it's an old belief or low self-worth. Maybe it's a story you picked up as a child. Often working with a therapist, reviewing what you wrote down in step one, or even working with an inner child meditation (there's one on my website) can help you identify such fears and stories. Sometimes a memory is so pertinent we immediately know where such fears stem from. Perhaps you experienced a time when such a big choice didn't turn out as planned, resulting in a story being concocted about what that meant (like you're lazy and don't know how to make big decisions).

Consider who may benefit from such worries (hint: it's probably some shadow part of you). How have these stories kept you small, safe or off the hook – because when you don't have to try, then you can't fail. But, you also can't succeed.

3. Work through changes

Now you know the beliefs, stories and limitations keeping you from your desires, you can actively change them. Questioning a belief is a sure-fire way to dislodge its grip. Try listing all the alternative meanings you could attach to your past, yourself or the things that you believe are limiting you. For example, when a relationship ends, we could make a story that says we weren't worthy of love, or not pretty enough, or not good enough for the other person. Or, we could create alternative meanings, like:

- we simply grew apart

- we learned all we could learn together

- this partner wasn't ready for all of me.

The meaning we choose to apply holds great power. Choose wisely.

As your old self-limiting stories crumble, replace them with new, more loving ones. Try positive affirmations, visualising your desires or future scripting (where you write the story of your future the way you intend for it to be and then read it as often as you can, ideally daily). More than that, work with your energy to clear your way into higher vibrations. This might involve regular chakra clearing and maintenance through meditation (there's a chakra-balancing meditation on my website), yoga, psychic cord cutting or any other modality you intuitively feel drawn to. Seek out help to work through your internal world if you need to. This might include focusing (as intuitively guided) on each of your physical, mental, emotional and spiritual layers with the appropriate help. For example, you may find a personal trainer for your body and mind, a therapist or coach for your mind and emotions, and an energy worker for your energy field. Intuitively check in when it's time to shake that up, too.

4. What do you really want?

This might seem obvious, but knowing what you *really* want isn't always so easy. Not everyone has familiarised themselves with their personal preferences, or felt allowed to entertain them. This is especially true for women. Consider all the ways you previously denied what you wanted (and perhaps work through the meaning you attached to this). Who else in your life has told you that you can't? Does that need to be true for you?

Know what you want – and then *believe* it's possible for you. Procrastination highlights fears. Sometimes we are simply scared of being who we really are and receiving what it is we really want. This may not be an issue of indecision, but instead a lack of connection with yourself, your truth and your own power. Confidently choosing and deciding requires clarity of desire and a wholehearted belief that you are allowed to receive – then accepting full receivership when it arrives.

What if?

Q *Help! I feel stuck. I need to make some big decisions and I don't know which way to go. Should I further my education (and attempt another degree) or switch to another job in another industry? Both require time and effort, but I want to minimise the impact on my future career and earnings. I don't want to waste time, especially if I only change my mind later. Can I make a wrong choice? And, if I do, can I then fix it?*

+⁺.⁺ˑ ˑ

A Constantly questioning 'What if?' signals a lack of self-belief, and not knowing who we are and what we really want makes choice quite hard. Because all of life is a choice, we must be clear on what we want in order to receive it.

Knowing what you want is not so much how you want it to *look* or about mitigating all the potential pitfalls, but more about how you want to *feel*. How do you want to *express* who you are? How do you want to *experience* the world? This desired feeling provides a barometer for your choices. Will a choice bring you closer to, or further away from, that feeling? Your body signals which steps to take, which direction to move in. Follow the feeling, not the mind's interpretation or anticipation of the outcome.

What if you saw this so very differently? What if every possible outcome could still serve you, still be good for you (albeit in ways your mind may not understand)? What if your experience was perfect, simply because it's here? When we see all of life as supporting us, we see every moment – and choice – as a gift. Such gifts beget gratitude for the choices and opportunities before you. Suddenly, the gravity of your choice lessens, as there is always something else to choose from – an abundance of choice and experience, rather than a fixed solution with only one guaranteed outcome.

While it feels like some choices are more important, or unequally weighted, it's actually the *outcomes* that may have different impacts, not the choice itself. The process of choosing should remain the same, no matter the outcome. But our minds see it differently, wanting to guarantee us things it simply has no business promising (namely, a promised solution of its own control and making). Because no outcome can ever truly be guaranteed, you cannot really get it wrong. You can only choose. And if you arrive somewhere you don't want to be, you are free to choose again. The attachment and weight of the outcomes you desire may require a different perspective, though.

No matter the choice, you will learn what you need to learn. You can choose to learn it in this job, or that job. This relationship, or that relationship. But the underlying soul lesson will still turn up, no matter which decision you take.

Sliding doors

Q *I loved the movie* Sliding Doors *with Gwyneth Paltrow and I've wondered if that's how life really works. Can we really end up in some parallel universe by missing the train or simply making some wrong choice? I've heard the idea that what is meant for us cannot pass us by, but I feel like I am always being passed by, or being passed over. There are loads of decisions I regret – like staying too long in a relationship, or not taking a job or making a move sooner – and I can't help wonder if things would have all turned out so very differently if I'd made that other choice. Can we miss what's meant for us and end up on some other life path?*

A Oh, what complexity we miss in our pop culture and memes. The sentiment 'what is meant for you cannot pass you by' is often shared; what's not as shareable is 'what is meant for you cannot pass you by, because your soul lessons and purpose will ensure it turns up no matter what you choose, but the classroom may change'. Nope, not as shareable, but arguably more accurate.

What is meant for you may not be the specific job/partner/ event – but the *lesson* they'd present. What is meant for you is the path of growth your soul agreed to ahead of time, and where and how you learn those lessons is left to the choose-your-own-adventure of your free will. What is meant for you is the lesson, so the lesson cannot pass you by.

So, if you're meant to experience love, it will come.

If you're meant to experience wealth, it will come.

If you're meant to experience forgiveness, it will come.

But the how – and even the when and where – is not necessarily up to you. This detail isn't set in stone and is indeed the subject of so many variables, a bit like which train Gwyneth does or does not get on.

Not every minor detail of your life is pre-determined; it's not fixed in stone. Many timelines and possibilities, far beyond what our minds may entertain as viable options, exist when following your soul path. Your choices may dictate which alternative outcome becomes available to you – what if Gwyneth walked or got a bus or a taxi instead of that train?! – but each alternative outcome will still ensure you learn what you need to learn. The lesson doesn't change even if the context does.

Your choices influence where, when and how you end up experiencing what you're here to experience. And when you follow your gut instincts, you're more likely to end up in the right place at the right time, not just for what your ego desires, but for what your soul requires for growth.

As for regrets, please forgive yourself. Regret is a powerful emotion signalling you can simply choose better next time.

Ask the regret what it's here to teach you. Does your regret point you towards what you really want, or to what you can do differently next time?

If you were truly meant to leave the relationship earlier you would have; you stayed because you weren't ready to go. Therein lies the lesson.

If you were truly ready to take that job, you would have said 'yes'. Instead, the 'no' taught you something else. Value that.

And if you were truly meant to move sooner, then you may have missed everything else you experienced to prompt the eventual move. You needed it, at a soul level, even though your human self may never come to understand it as such.

Things may indeed have turned out differently if you'd left that relationship, taken that job or moved on sooner – and you would not be who you are now. And who you are now is perfect and exactly where you need to be. There is no alternative universe where *you* would suddenly be better. You are perfect, now.

QUESTIONS TO ASK YOURSELF

You might like to meditate on the following questions, use them as journalling prompts, invite your own SST to answer you, or turn an oracle card from The Little Sage Oracle Cards in response.

* What do I really desire most in my life right now?
* What does my head (or ego) have to say on this desire or on my decisions?
* What does my intuition feel about these choices?
* What's really holding me back from making the choices I want to make in my life?
* How can I work through these limitations?

If these questions and answers prompt a deeper enquiry, I've compiled a list of additional resources at helenjacobs. co/ask.

Unsticking stuckness

Realising we have choices, we can soon begin to wonder *how*. How can I get unstuck? How can I escape this sticky situation and find one that feels better? How do I let go of what's not working and cultivate what is? We are quick to reach for the better feeling without recognising what the 'stuckness' is teaching us.

Feeling stuck is actually a good sign (I promise!). It suggests we need to change where we are, either by leaving or tweaking how we perceive the situation. Changing the story we're telling ourselves about the situation we're in, or the person involved, is often enough to help us see things differently. But it's still only one step. Feeling stuck can feel like we're in quicksand – and when the ego alone tries to lead us out, we can end up sinking even more. Spirit has a very different escape route when it comes to getting unstuck. And it's not always what we hoped it would be.

Other times, we stick out such a situation because we cannot fathom something beyond our current experience. Better the devil you know, right? Well, no. You don't have to lie with the devil; you can expand into infinite possibilities if you're simply willing to imagine them. It's often hard to be reminded that we must believe it in order to see it. We'd all the more rather see it to believe it (but I've just managed to sneak that in and remind you, anyway!). What is possible for you on the other side of your stuckness is the brilliance you can imagine for yourself; but if you can't entertain that as possible *for you*, then it won't be.

Many of my personal questions to Chris (more than I'd care to admit) have focused on how to clear the way to something better, as have many of the questions I've asked for friends. I include a smattering of examples here, with the hope they shed light for you, too. In truth, all of our questions are looking to 'something better' or 'something more', so, in that way, this is a shorter chapter, for the whole book is pointing us towards unsticking our 'stuckness', and moving more freely in the expanse of our new opportunities.

Getting unstuck

Q *My life feels like it's groundhog day. I'm stuck in a rut and change seems so overwhelming. I'm unhappy at work and my relationships are a bit ho-hum. I'm perennially single and keep attracting the wrong partners. My days are spent giving to others and there's little, if anything, left for me at the end of the day. I don't think it's that I'm depressed, more just a bit flat, like I don't really have any zest for anything in my life anymore. I'm worried this is it for me. Is it?*

A Your feelings are trying to wake you up to new possibilities. Are you listening?

Acknowledging that this feels bad is the first step. Done! You don't have to continue choosing this for yourself, and you don't need to know what's next, yet.

First, clear these feelings and the heavier energy so they pass, before you reach for what feels better. (So, put down the comfort food and prepare to tackle this head on. I'm about to show you how to work with your physical, mental, emotional and energetic bodies to do just that.) You'll be the best judge of whether you need additional support – you may want to rule out depression with a health professional first.

Feeling flat may require processing at deeper levels. I teach the importance of clearing, healing and restoring ourselves physically, mentally, emotionally and energetically, but that can also be a tall order when you feel so terribly flat. Start with baby steps towards feeling better, even if it's simply listening to your favourite song or doing an activity that floods you with happiness. When you've mustered more mojo, you'll have more oomph to tackle the deeper underlying factors that led you here. Juicing yourself up isn't about quick external fixes (yes, I really meant put down that comfort food); instead focus on the things that bring you joy. Simple pleasures will help jolt that heavier energy. (And, by the way, reaching all too often for those quick fixes such as food, alcohol and distraction may very well have been slowly contributing to your groundhog day to begin with.)

Being stuck can often signal you've lost touch with what makes you *you*. Somewhere along the line you lost yourself and landed in this rut. Your deeper level exploration will help you understand why, but that may take some time. While processing, simultaneously reconnect with yourself – your inner world, your interests and your passions. Life wants to jolt you with a defibrillator, if you'll only call for help. Revisit what you loved to do as a child. Run, play, dance, sing, draw, paint, create. Start here. Try classes. Try new things. This new stimulus will bring you new people, new places, new beginnings. Try one new thing each week, then a few times a week, and then every day. Change your route to work. Try cooking different meals. Listen to new music and podcasts.

These are your defibrillators.

Of course, by themselves, these aren't the answer. But they will bring a little spark into your days and weeks, which will soon add up. And it will add up to just enough for you to tackle the bigger questions you haven't yet asked out loud. Understanding why you've made the choices that led you here can help.

With a little increase in energy, you can then ask this feeling what it wants you to know. Normally, it's a sign we've stayed too long in our current circumstances. But it can also prompt you to consider if you believe there could be more than this for you. Or it might nudge you into deeper levels of self-love and self-belief by asking you to want more for yourself. Do the deeper work of excavating your stories and limiting beliefs to remove this inner world construct, so you won't become stuck again. Journalling, working with a therapist, or simply embarking on a spirit-led journey of self-discovery can initiate such deep work.

There is a whole new life awaiting you. But first you must choose to let this one go. The only way out of a rut is out, one small step at a time.

All I've known

Q *I'm recently divorced from my second husband, a marriage that began soon after my first husband died. I've been in relationships ever since I was young, and I'm nearing the later years of my life now. Finally, for the first time in my life, I don't feel I need a partner, but I've never been alone before. I don't know how to manage a bank account, or get my own place. I've suddenly woken up in a foreign world and I'm not sure how to exist here. I never had children, and many of my friends and I parted ways when I remarried. How do I start over this late in life? What do I do now when all I've ever known is gone, but I don't know what's next?*

A Starting over is never easy, no matter your physical age. We all need to move through our lessons sooner or later, and become who we came here to be.

Spirit shows me this is a period of significant change, not just in the outer world as you find a new home, new friends and new community, but in your inner world. This is an exciting time of personal and spiritual growth. You are embarking on the most meaningful relationship you'll ever know: with *yourself.*

You know more about yourself than you *think* you do. But you have not given yourself credit for all that you have done in your life, in your marriages, in the life you've already lived. You have not seen yourself through the eyes of those who love you, for you have not fully loved yourself. This is the greatest adventure that awaits you.

This moment in your life is a coming of age, a coming out, a rite of passage. This is about freedom and truly savouring the richness of a life you've been craving. Chris shows me you've fared well financially; this isn't a time for you to worry about money. With your financial security, it's meant to be a time to reclaim your power, to use the available resources to live the life you always secretly craved. There is a wildness here, bubbling beneath the surface. Do not squander what life has given you.

You will need to push outside your comfort zone. Join those classes. Take that trip. Take those risks. Honour your nomadic nature. A long life spent stifling yourself for your parents, your partners, for others, has snuffed out your inner flame. Let your inner rebel revolt! Free yourself from someone else's ideas for life; now it's time to create your own.

Dream. Expand your ideas of what is possible for you. Entertain the idea there could be multiple lovers, friends and comrades. Travel, explore and take it all in. Why limit yourself to what you feel has been safe, when you can liberate yourself into a world of wonder and possibility? It's just waiting for you to take the first step.

There is a lifetime of liberation, expression and freedom – a wild woman to entertain – that a younger you wasn't yet ready to dream of.

QUESTIONS TO ASK YOURSELF

You might like to meditate on the following questions, use them as journalling prompts, invite your own SST to answer you, or turn an oracle card from The Little Sage Oracle Cards in response.

* What emotions or physical sensations are present in your body right now?
* Ask these emotions or sensations why they are here. What do they want you to know?
* What stories are you telling yourself about your life or certain situations right now? What might happen if you changed those stories?

If these questions and answers prompt a deeper enquiry, I've compiled a list of additional resources at helenjacobs. co/ask.

Work, work, work

Perhaps because my own career trajectory took such a sudden and surprising twist – from PR executive to psychic – I attract many people with questions about their jobs, career and purpose. In some ways it feels like the world is catching up to early predictions Chris made regarding the nature of our workplaces and work structures, which are dramatically changing. I remember when I first left PR to give psychic readings, no one worked remotely. Co-working places were non-existent in my town, as was any demand for homes built with work spaces in mind. And yet, thrust into that new lifestyle, Chris convinced me it would become the norm.

Back then, Chris would describe (for me and for clients) what he called a 'portfolio lifestyle' – multiple projects, flexible work hours and location-independent work. I remember more than one client looking at me disbelievingly when I would describe this new work mode to them. Now, several years (and a global pandemic) later, this has become the norm.

Similarly, about the same time, I relayed to many clients that I saw them writing, taking photos and sharing them via what looked like a magazine, but wasn't. Nor was it a blog or Facebook, which was taking off about that time. Whatever this thing was, I told these clients they would benefit greatly and it would contribute to – in some cases quite significantly, or even replace – their income levels. Turns out, this was Instagram (if only Chris had told me how to create it, monetise it and subsequently sell it to Zuckerberg). Who knew so many businesses, including my own, would explode with such an invention? We're poised for more to come.

In a post-COVID-19 world, career trajectories, workplaces and entire industries are thrust into change and the jobs our children will have don't even exist yet. In this chapter are Chris's answers to the typical questions I've received about our work, jobs and vocation – which we cannot confuse with our purpose. Our purpose is more than what we *do* in the world; our purpose is remembering who we came here to *be*. Post-pandemic, the world may look a little different, but our true purpose still remains, perhaps now more important than before.

Like a boss

Q *My boss is the boss from hell. She arrived about eighteen months ago from our overseas head office. At first I was thrilled to hear I'd report to a woman – I am keen to grow and learn from women in leadership positions, especially as I'm one of the few women in my department – but she's been anything but a dream. I've been with this firm for ten years, slowly moving up the ranks. I hit every sales target, meet every KPI, but she's never pleased. Team culture has significantly shifted and team members are now leaving. After all this time, I never thought I'd leave, but I cannot see a way forward now as she's a boulder in my path. What should I do?*

A Sometimes life brings us roadblocks, or people-shaped boulders, to redirect our course. I believe this is one such time. When facing a block, we are invited to see the situation as if it were a mirror, highlighting back to us what we can change, or heal, within ourselves. I call this the Mirror Technique. I go deeper into this concept in *You Already Know*, but you'll find a guide to the technique on page 257.

The **Mirror Technique** asks you to identify what is triggering you, then look inward to identify where you may hold a similar belief, or how you could reposition your perception of what is triggering you, thus creating an internal shift.

The Mirror Technique came from Chris as a process to help us reposition others and events as a way of seeing ourselves with a new perspective. What if your boss was simply reflecting existing feelings where *you* are never pleased with your own achievements? Are there areas of your life where your communication isn't clear? What does this woman trigger inside of you? And what if that has more to do with you than it does her? That's not to say that this situation isn't true and real; rather, taking a different look at the situation can produce different results.

You are not going to change your boss. Please do not waste precious energy trying. Nor do I think she's in a hurry to go elsewhere, so please don't try to wait her out. This is not about creating bosses, colleagues and workplaces that meet you where *you* are, but rather allowing you to learn more about yourself from the cultures and environments you're in. And if you don't like the environment, move.

The biggest clue this mirror reflects is your desire for a mentor. Your boss is highlighting for you a latent desire.

Rather than expecting her to fill that position for you, why not take the reins and create that for yourself, and others? I say others because Chris shows me that you will play a vital role for other women in business, showing them a new way to be in business, to be the example in leadership you are looking and longing for yourself, most likely in stark contrast to your boss's mode of operation. When viewed in this way, I'd say your boss is offering you a great gift, wouldn't you? Without her arrival, you may never have realised this about yourself.

Complaining and wishing the situation was different won't catalyse change. *You* will create change. This is your sign to course-correct. After ten years of meeting all the KPIs and targets, it might now be time for new ones.

You wanted your career to go a certain way; you had certain expectations about your time at this organisation and what might be 'owed' to you there. But there is something deeper here to learn, if you look more closely. Your boss is showing you all the ways you've outgrown this organisation, its offerings and its career path for you. Clarify the type of mentor you desire – then task yourself with finding them and, indeed, becoming them. Our world is looking for new leadership and new ways of doing business. You are at the helm for this.

Life knew this before you did, and has slowly been edging you towards another path. It's time to move on.

Going online

Q *I hate my job and am tempted to follow the online bandwagon. I'm currently an HR manager and I just turn up every day for the money. I dislike my colleagues and the work I do. It's awful. When I started out in HR I wanted to create meaningful workplaces and cultures, I wanted to help people in their work, because it's such a big part of their lives. But I can't even do that for myself.*

I am considering doing something online. I've got a few business ideas I think could make money, mainly importing stuff from China and reselling it. My husband isn't so keen on me leaving my job for this because a few years ago I attempted running an online kids' clothing store but I couldn't figure it out. We only sold a few items and now there's this huge inventory I can't sell. I'm not tech savvy and don't really want to waste time learning how to run an online business – but can I afford not to? Isn't this where the world is heading?

Maybe I should study? I don't really want to start over. What work am I meant to be doing? Are these ideas going to help me get ahead or am I going to be stuck doing this dead-end job forever?

A Sure, Instagram makes it look like everyone is living by the beach and making money in their sleep, but curated looks can be deceiving. Tempting as an online business may be, Chris shows me it isn't necessarily the viable financial option you hope it to be for you. Don't despair! Spirit also has something else in store ... however, it requires we venture *into* the resistance, not run from it.

Whoever sold us the lie that money will make us happy? Do you really want to just make a quick buck (online or otherwise), or are you really more interested in meaningful work that can also pay the bills? And before you vote for the quick buck, please ask yourself: then what? You'd just have more money and still be unfulfilled. Sure, your passion hasn't panned out to date, but that can change. Your desire to not start again in either your career or finances is important here, too. Your mind is simply trying to add one idea to the other, but it's creating errors in calculations.

Online businesses, particularly product based, require significant investment of capital, time and knowledge to conquer this ever-changing market and technology. There's nothing quick about a win here for you. Instead, the opportunity lies much closer to home.

HR called to your desire to help others be happy in their work. And here you are, miserable in your own. This is what Chris would call a beautiful intersection of lessons and purpose – even if you perceive it more like the intersection of a rock and a hard place. Our soul's purpose and lessons are intrinsically entwined; by learning our lessons we develop our purpose – and I see your purpose is indeed helping others find happiness in their work and workplaces. The goal here, then, isn't to run away, but to go in deeper – there's a goldmine here for you, if you're willing to dig deep.

Let's entertain a little psychic prediction: I see you establishing your own business, perhaps coaching or a consultancy rather than a traditional HR firm. You'll deeply guide your clients through a more personal journey in relation to their work. This is not bland professional development. Instead, you'll support and mentor others to reconcile this same grievance in their lives. But, first, you must reconcile it within yourself.

You are about to be your own best case study. You are going to coach yourself through career change and transition. Record your process, and then you will coach others through the same transformation. HR was just a stepping stone, not the whole picture, and you're about to add more strings to your bow.

You weren't too far off the mark considering moving online – but as a service offering. The location-independent element offers the freedom you are craving.

One last point: the inventory you're holding may simply be a sunk cost, or you may be able to quickly move it through eBay or similar. This may fund future study into coaching or online business training. There is an alternative job in HR in the meantime, as you set this up. You'll be happier running your own show with the skill set (and purpose) that is truly yours. From there, you will help many other people also find what their special skill set is. Good luck!

Dazzling brilliance

Q *For the past ten years I've worked for myself, consulting and freelance writing while I raised my kids. I've had some success and built up a loyal client base but I'm getting bored and can feel the life draining out of me. I want to take on bigger, more exciting projects but I don't think I can do it all while still juggling random work hours around my kids' schedules. Now my kids are getting older, I'd like to expand this freelance model to more of an agency by hiring other mums for flexible hours so I can take on more of the exciting, bigger projects. I'd have to raise my rates and possibly alienate my current clientele I've worked so hard for. Is this possible, or should I just be happy where I am as it is working? Could I grow this business without burning out further?*

A Feeling the life draining out of you is a pretty good sign change is needed. Sustaining the status quo will only further deplete you, making it even harder to address later. Over-staying your welcome, whether in work, relationships, habits and so on, stagnates energy and stymies growth. In an ever-expanding world, you, too, must keep moving and expanding. Staying somewhere your spirit is unhappy is not good for anyone – not for your kids, not for your clients and especially not for you. Denying yourself the pleasure of receiving the life you desire also denies others your true brilliance and their pleasure in receiving *that* version of you (and your work).

Imagine what it might feel like if all your dreams came true. Could you receive all those riches? Could you allow yourself to receive a life that was vibrant, exciting and engaging? Could you deem yourself worthy of that? Let go of the expectations of how you *should* be working and what suits your kids and clients. Your yearning heralds in something far more wondrous and magical, if only you learn to receive it. Imagine modelling this for your children, too.

Why stay in familiar discomfort? Is it because you:

- don't believe you can have what you want?

- don't believe you could succeed?

- are scared?

- think you'd have to work so much harder to make something else happen?

Recognising your fear is important; then, you can reduce its grip on you (you don't need to eradicate your fear to act). Take time to work through this to give yourself the best shot.

Have you ever wondered why you desire what you do and someone else desires something entirely different? Chris shows me that, just as Rumi said, what you seek is also seeking you – your desires are not just random longings, but actual guidance. What you desire is not just possible, but *inevitable*. Dreaming of expanding your business isn't just a daydream, but guidance that an expanded business is trying to make its way to you. Your task, then, is to learn how to get out of your own way to receive it. What if all you had to do to receive this new life was let go of the heaviness you've been carrying?

There's inner work to be done to receive what is hurtling towards you. Expand into your new possibilities by expanding your self-belief (and then back it up energetically). Reinforce your energy, your power and your presence. To do this, you could work with your chakras, locate your power and weave it through your system. For example, supporting your throat and sacral chakras will enhance expression and creativity, while supporting your solar plexus chakra will strengthen your internal power.

There is a strength that wants to be transmitted and expressed from you – find your voice, know your worth and communicate this with the world. Through your prices, through your hiring choices and through the financial success you (and others) can then enjoy. You'll pay it forward; this isn't about money for money's sake, it's about what else you can invest in when you have it.

Do not be afraid of your own brilliance. Be afraid of who you might become if you deny it.

CHAKRAS

Chakras are energy centres located throughout the body and its surrounding energy field. I think of them as an energetic digestive system. When working well, they absorb, transmute and expel energy as it moves through our system. As such, we want to keep them clear and healthy so we can maintain energetic vitality. Blocked or stagnant energy can create blockages in our emotional, mental and physical bodies.

Working with your own chakras may look like a regular chakra-balancing meditation (there's one on my website) or working with a practitioner for a treatment such as reiki. Yoga poses work with different chakras, and different sounds (frequencies), crystals and even essential oils can all positively affect the chakras. Awareness of the themes you're working on in your life can correlate with particular chakras, just as you may energetically perceive your chakras (or notice physical ailments in their physical location), which can point to what may need healing in your life. I've included more about the seven main chakras on page 265 for you to explore.

#lifegoals

Q *I'm approaching early retirement and can proudly say I've accomplished most of my life goals, both professionally and personally. I never married and never had kids (never wanted to), so I've saved my cash and have a strong investment portfolio. This was always the plan: work hard, retire early and enjoy my later years travelling and enjoying the good life. Trouble is, right now I can't travel anyway and my friends aren't available to join me. What's the point if there's no one to enjoy it with? What do I do now I've fulfilled everything I sought out to achieve? Maybe I don't want to retire – but what's next? A great love? A new passion to pursue? What do I do when I feel I've done all I came here to do?*

A How marvellous you've achieved all you wanted to! Congratulations! Celebrate. Really, *really* celebrate and take this in. Marinate in this accomplishment; your gratitude for what is here prepares the soil for what comes next (perhaps it's pertinent to note I originally misspelled 'soil' as 'soul' – you'll prepare that, too).

Freeing yourself from the burden of living a life bound by circumstance draws us closer to spirit's perspective; spirit never sees us as beholden to our bank accounts, or societal expectations, or anything else our minds convince us to live up to. Perhaps for the first time in your life, you can now answer the question 'What do I really want?' in earnest. With true financial freedom, you are given a great opportunity to entertain deeper questions: who are you and what are you here to do and be? We can ask these questions at any time, but, sadly, many wait for such financial freedom and lose the chance of being spiritually free in the process.

Chris shares a clairvoyant image: a farmer overlooking his fields. This farmer has enjoyed an extended summer and harvested a bumper crop. Now, it's time to clear the fields – how bittersweet to let go of all that came before. There's a timing at play here. The farmer doesn't rush to plant the next season's crops; he trusts that time will come. To a passer-by, the soil lays dormant, unproductive. But the farmer knows it's actively recovering. The soil (and, again, it was misspelled as soul) is turned, aerated and fertilised before new seeds are planted and bloom.

Don't rush into anything new; aerate the soil (or soul, as the case may be). Try new things. New classes. New ideas. New books, topics, people. Stimulate yourself in new ways and discover what sparks joy in you. You might just surprise yourself. And you're creating a rich, fertile ground as you do. The farmer sows many seeds, knowing not all seeds will take. Not everything planted will bloom. Watch for what takes hold in your life. New life will be born out of this, but it's too early to tell which seeds will bloom.

Engaging with your life this way, new friendships will form and Chris says you'll also move house. There may indeed be the great love of your life – that's not the goal, but a beautiful by-product of what you're planting here. The absence of goals is kind of the goal!

Chris also shows me a new way to invest, not just in assets, but in people, ideas and businesses. Why plant just one seed when you can plant and nurture an entire orchard? May your harvest not just feed you this season, but for all seasons to come. May your legacy be that your harvest was not just for you at all, but for an entire village for many seasons more.

Future (work)forces

Q *I've lost my job as a result of the COVID-19 pandemic. I am also just finishing up my studies (I had been lucky enough to get a job before I had completed my degree). The world seems so unstable. I'm nervous that there's so much unemployment, and people won't want to leave their secure jobs, making my employment and career prospects pretty hopeless. It also seems like workforces are changing so much – I don't even know what it would be like to start a career with working remotely. How would I network, receive mentorship and grow contacts for career advancement? I'm really nervous about my career and the future of the workforce. What's in store for my generation's career paths?*

A Losing jobs, security and the prospect of a guaranteed future career is really rough and it's worth giving yourself time to feel all the feelings this might bring up. (The chapter on loss later in this book might also help. See page 123.)

Workforces have undeniably changed, not only as a result of this pandemic, but as technology has increased and advanced over the past decade or two. Gone are the days of long-term employment or one job – let alone one career path! – for life. While it may feel so unstable and unclear at the outset of your career, spirit sees this very differently.

Spirit wants to remind us of this: *we choose the experience of the reality we live in.*

Let me explain. There are absolutely very real external circumstances here, such as the pandemic, economic consider-ations and unemployment figures, for example. We cannot deny these realities. What spirit is referring to here, then, is not that these realities don't exist, but rather our perception of them is a far bigger determinate of our *experience* of these realities. How we perceive the limitations of the external world and what we choose to do about it are far more important than the situations themselves. We can choose to see ourselves as limited by this, or we can choose to see it as working for us, not against us. Opportunity, not just beauty, is in the eye of the beholder.

This change in the workforce will compel us to reconsider the nature of work and employment, hopefully coming back to our soul mission more than the notion of simply working for regular pay. In a simple way, we are now challenging the outdated notion of a standard nine-to-five workday and even a five-day working week. When we need to create more stillness, space and silence in our days, such a tweak can have far-reaching positive repercussions.

Taking a bigger-picture view of the nature of workforces and purpose, spirit has long been suggesting through my work that our individual soul paths must come to the fore more than our preoccupation with occupation. We must begin to remember the bigger *why* – our soul mission and life purpose – and let this be the driving force of what we do, and who we are here to be, in the world. When we allow the two to meet, we'll have found the new sweet spot for our workplaces.

There is an opportunity here to draw on your own unique skills, talents and interests – not just at an intellectual level, but at the soul level. It's not by chance that these changes are coinciding with the advent of technological advances. It's easier than ever before to work remotely, forge your own career path and even start your own business. The longer-term view here is that we will indeed move away from such structured, hierarchical, even patriarchal business structures into a more 'feminine' model of business – one that is more collaborative, organic, flat, intuitive and innovative. A younger generation not only stands to benefit from that, but is tasked with helping to create it.

In the short term, your career may not start out as you had hoped, or how it started for those who went before you, but I also feel like that may be the point.

While we are waiting for our soul's purpose to reveal itself (and even if it never becomes a profit-driven decision for us), we will still contribute. There is still work for you to do, to contribute and to be a part of – whether in your industry of study or elsewhere. Sometimes the plan we held in our heads, the expectations we had of our life path, or career path, can be infinitely limited in comparison with what the universe has in store for us.

You will be provided for. There will be work for you – and you've already demonstrated your employability by finding work before completing your studies. This moment in time may be teaching you adaptability, flexibility and how to become a creative problem-solver – all valuable skills to a potential employer, especially as the nature of our workplaces is going to demand them. You're actually poised ready to lead. You just haven't seen it as such yet.

. ✦ ˙

QUESTIONS TO ASK YOURSELF

You might like to meditate on the following questions, use them as journalling prompts, invite your own SST to answer you, or turn an oracle card from The Little Sage Oracle Cards in response.

* What do the current situations or relationships in my life mirror back to me?
* What might I learn if I changed within myself what I identify in others? Or if I celebrate within myself what I celebrate in others?
* What do I most want to contribute to the world via my work?
* Complete this sentence: If money were no object and I could fulfil my heart's true desire, I'd want to work as _____.

If these questions and answers prompt a deeper enquiry, I've compiled a list of additional resources at helenjacobs. co/ask.

. ✦ ˙

Money-go-round

What would you draw if I asked for a visual representation of how money makes the world go round? I imagine a picture showing how money swirls, flows, shifts, rises, falls and accumulates, before circulating again. If also asked to draw how energy flows, my pictures would be almost identical.

Countless times I've asked my clients what the source of their money is. Many say it's their employers, their clients, their bank account. And then I inevitably ask, 'But, how does it get there? Where did it come from to get into our bank accounts?' The conversation tends to focus on what we need to *do* to have money arrive in said accounts. And, this is all very logical, but also a very limited way to think about money and where it comes from. Just like when my children ask me where babies comes from (putting *the talk* aside), I could simply focus on the multiplication from the parents – but we could trace that baby all the way back to the source. And let's face it, I'm a big-picture kind of person.

When it comes to money, just like most things in life, I'm more interested in the energy *behind* it. I'm not so interested in the immediate step before its arrival in my hands, but tracing it all the way back, to a source greater than my bank account, or my business – where did it come from before then? And, what's the driving force behind its flow to me?

From an abundance mindset and a higher energetic frequency, I see money as an ever-expanding stockpile. This ever-abundant pile of money then swirls, flows, shifts, rises, falls and accumulates, not just at the stockpile, but in all the other places that money has circulated to (like, say, my bank account). In financial terms, money continually grows because of things like compounding interest. But as I'm not a financial expert, rather an energetic one, I see our money much like I see our universe and our energy: ever-expanding, stemming from an ever-abundant source. And knowing how energetic laws work, I can relate to my money so very differently.

Just as your true source of energy is not your body, but some higher state that is the source of all life force, so, too, the source of your money is not just what's in your bank account, but it comes from the source of all money … because, when you picture that diagram of just how money circulates, it all comes from the same original source, from which it then multiplies and circulates.

Our rapid move towards a cashless society helps us wrap our heads around the idea that money isn't just paper (or plastic) and coins. Its value isn't so much in the material itself, but the value we attribute to it, based on our understanding and beliefs about what money can do for us. And, if money is no longer seen as physical but increasingly more electronic, we can see what we are really exchanging is value. And, I would argue a step further, what we are really exchanging is *energy*.

Our personal vibration is an energetic set point affecting the flow of energy in, around and out of our lives. What happens on the inside affects the outside flow, so the frequency of our thoughts, actions and practices with money can affect the way it flows through our life. How we value ourselves and the beliefs we hold about money, what it is and where it comes from affect our relationship to it. Change your energy, you change the flow of money to you.

However you visualise the world's money-go-round, we usually just want more of it. Money is a hot topic asked by many friends and this chapter shares a snippet of Chris's thoughts on how money flows, where it really comes from and how we can shift our relationship to it, thus attracting more of it. We're also reminded not just to accumulate money for our own ego's sense of safety or power, but to keep circulating it in ways that have meaning and value for us and our world.

At the core, we can all have money flow to us, but we will each have different soul lessons around money, and a different purpose with money. It is not money that defines our value, but our values that define how we attract, circulate and give our money, especially as our world moves into its new energetic reality.

Financially fucked

Q *Will I ever reach my financial goals? I mostly live from pay to pay. I know I'm meant to be saving, but anytime I get a little bit of money together it seems to vanish. I worry about my future. Am I ever going to be able to buy my own home? Will I have to work for my entire life, because retirement feels so impossible? I'm single, so I don't have the support or backing of anyone else and sometimes I think this makes everything else so much harder. Am I always going to be financially fucked?*

A Take a deep breath and, just for a minute, let's entertain a completely different way of thinking about things. Chris sees finances and money so very differently than we mere humans do, so bear with me as we explore a few concepts here.

Somewhere along the line, we conflated and confused money for safety and security. Of course, in our capitalist society, we need money, but this isn't the *true source* of our safety and security. Energy is. When we feel *energetically* safe and secure, we have a strong foundation for all other forms of safety. But, first, let's address the physical aspect of money.

An absence of money sends our nervous system into a very real fight-or-flight response. We panic and our brain responds in the same way as if we were in physical danger. We may not have a sabre-toothed tiger chasing us, but we feel just as threatened. And it can be a tad difficult to be Zen – and in an abundance mindset – while feeling threatened.

Explore the (often free) financial supports available to help you with financial education, such as financial literacy courses and clever saving tips. Knowledge is power. Understanding your money at a physical level will shift your relationship to it, reducing the stress and restoring calm.

With this foundation, we can move beyond the physicality of money to the mental level. This requires a deep exploration of your stories, beliefs and limitations around money. For example, believing money will 'vanish', 'slip through your fingers' or 'pay everyone else's bills before your own' is a self-fulfilling prophecy. Change the belief and you change the outcome.

To put it bluntly, you're financially fucked because you believe you are.

Beyond the physical and mental, we must then explore the emotional and energetic layers. Our energetic set point is the sum of our intentions, thoughts, beliefs, emotions and actions, so when it comes to money, it is attracted – and repelled – based on your energetic set point.

Here are some suggested steps to take:

- Clear and strengthen your energy centres, particularly your base chakra. For example, try visualising red light pouring into the base of your spine, then moving up and down through your spine and down to the earth.

- Cut and clear energy cords with money stories. Task your SST to disconnect psychic cords connecting you to your debt or past financial decisions and stressors. They will clairvoyantly look like umbilical cords between you and the object or situation. If you need further help visualising and energetically enacting this, I have a cutting cords meditation on my website.

- Release the emotions you've felt around money – fear, shame, loss and so on.

- Understand the intention and beliefs *behind* your financial goals by responding to questions like:

    ◆ Who controls your money?

    ◆ Where does your money come from?

    ◆ What is the true source of your money?

    ◆ What do you need to do for money to turn up?

- ◆ Can money turn up even if you do nothing?

- ◆ Is it possible for you to feel differently about your money?

- Entertain what else is possible for you – and how that might feel. Let's say it feels safe and secure, then that becomes your guiding feeling. Generate more of that feeling. When making choices, decide if it will bring you more of that guiding feeling or not. Cultivating a sense of safety and security (or however else you might want to feel) attracts more of it to you, thus changing your set point.

You are the source of your true safety and security. You are responsible for the flow of money in your life, not just because of what you do, but how you feel. Seeing yourself as a powerful conductor of money, you'll make better decisions, appreciate your money and allow it to be pleasurable. To that end, it is indeed possible to buy your own home, or any other major financial decisions you believe you can make. But make sure that's truly what you desire.

As for living from pay to pay, Chris reminds you that money can flow to you from many sources, your pay is just one such avenue. Where else can you allow money to flow to you? Like me, you've probably fantasised about winning the lotto – that's another potential avenue (but, alas, also an unlikely one to attract). We can win money, sell stuff, have a side business ... but we can also invest and have our money work *for us*. Expand your thinking to all the channels through which money can make its way to you, then task that money to multiply.

Unsubscribe

Q *Am I the only one tired of the idea of working hard, and keeping up with this capitalist treadmill the whole world is on? I want off. I want to pack up and go live in a commune, grow my own food and barter for goods I can't make myself. Life should be so much simpler: homes that don't contribute to climate change; a lifestyle and pace that's gentler on our earth; desires that don't drain resources. Surely if we all did this, our world would improve. Please tell me I'm not just romanticising this ideal. Would I actually survive living against the grain?*

A My friend, your (simple) palace awaits! You're not the only one dreaming of this, and you could indeed flourish. You've actually answered your own question – you can create a far simpler life for yourself.

Chris has shown me a future where many others will also move in this same direction, where a barter or share economy funds this more sustainable way of life. It's already emerging. But this doesn't have to only be a big-picture concept; it can also happen at the micro level you are now considering.

This new economy will require clarity of the role you're to play within it. How do you wish to contribute? What unique skills do you have to offer? What do you need to receive from others? To the soul level, this is the most simplistic, natural way of living. To give and receive who and what you really are. The world of spirit and soul rejoices!

Here's my prediction: you will indeed jump off this treadmill. But it may be less of a jump than a transition of sorts. This doesn't have to be a drastic all-or-nothing kind of deal, unless you really want it to be. You don't have to go totally off-grid. This can actually be achieved in the life you lead now, if you wanted it to be.

Small changes in your life can produce good momentum in this direction. Figure out what funds and resources you might need to accommodate yourself, to have what you need and how you might go about finding your community of like-minded people. You are not the only one, and you also don't need to figure it out on your own. In seeing how others have gone before you, you'll naturally find your community.

A far simpler, slower-paced life is possible, just as it is possible to remove the burden of oversubscribed living. So, unsubscribe. And keep unsubscribing until you find the rhythm your heart and soul desire.

I'm a thriver

Q *I am constantly stressed about money. I grew up in a household where we would often struggle for money. My folks worked really hard for basically minimum wage. There was always enough for food and clothes, but not much else (although I didn't really realise that until I was older).*

Both my wife and I have good, secure jobs. I'm sure our respective parents are happy to see their hard work paying off, enabling their children to experience more than they did (just as we want for our kids, too). But, no matter how much money comes in, I'm always worried we won't have enough, that it will run out or one of us will lose our income and we'll hit hard times, just like my parents did. Will I ever be able to relax into the idea that we are going to be okay financially? And will my parents be okay now in their retirement?

A Beyoncé's voice is ringing in my ears as she leads Destiny's Child into 'I'm a Survivor'. As much as I wish I had a personal audience with Beyoncé, this is just how Chris is relaying this message. I interpret this as a sign you are a survivor, you won't give up and you'll come out stronger, richer and wiser. But survivors often spend too much time in survival mode, which doesn't play nicely with your nervous system.

When you're in a constant state of stress, your energy (and nervous system) is under constant threat. You needn't only be a survivor; you can be a *thriver*. To do this, we need to move you from a fearful state into an expanded state of full receivership.

A soul-aligned action step, then, is to work on bringing calm to your nervous system (transcendental meditation and network spinal analysis might help) so you can shift from that fight-or-flight response into a state of peace.

Beyond your nervous system, you may also need to address your Four Bodies – the physical, mental, emotional and energetic layers.

The **Four Bodies**, our physical, mental, emotional and spiritual/energetic layers, are a rich source of intuitive data. Objectively perceiving the sensations and feelings of each layer provides intuitive information about ourselves and our surroundings. Each layer, or body, is interconnected; a block in one affects another. Clearing and healing the layers *is* the deep, internal work, liberating yourself to be freely and wholly soul-aligned. I detail the Four Bodies more fully in *You Already Know*, and work with my clients in my programs to observe and interpret the data in their Four Bodies. Additional explanations of each layer, and how to work with them, are included on page 259.

Your mental body, in particular, needs attention. Face these old beliefs, habits and behaviours born out of your childhood and absorbed from your family of origin. Beliefs about where money comes from, what you need to do to receive it, and how much of it there is to go around can all be replaced now; shift to believing that something else is possible for you, again, bringing peace to your nervous system. How does a *thriver* think and act?

To address your energy, I invite you to work with your chakras (your body's energy centres; see page 265). There is one such energy centre located at the base of your spine known as the base chakra. The base chakra processes energy related to our thoughts, beliefs, experiences and actions around safety and security, including our financial safety and security. You have never truly felt financially safe. By clearing the *energy* associated with this belief, you can begin to let new energy into your body; you can allow new emotions and feelings around money to arise; you can think differently about money and allow an abundance mindset to replace the scarcity or lacking mindset. And then your behaviours and material manifestation of money and its flow will change.

Going even deeper, you can address this at the soul level. Your soul chose to incarnate into this lifetime to heal karma from a previous lifetime. It's one of the reasons you chose your parents and the financial experience you did growing up.

Your soul is not truly meant to experience material hardship in this lifetime; it's a spill-over fear from a previous life. Soul-level healing – past-life regression or soul retrieval – may bring a deeper sense of peace and ease into your situation.

Past-life regression is a healing technique, best tried with a trained professional, that through hypnosis takes you into aspects of your soul's past lives. By exploring – and healing – the past life, you can heal past trauma, release yourself from karmic debts, or simply understand yourself and your soul better in this lifetime.

Soul retrieval occurs when a practitioner energetically retrieves or recalls lost fragments of a soul. This fragmentation or disassociation may occur if a soul encounters trauma or pain in its physical body, or has not integrated energies into physical form. When a soul makes a vow or contract it has not released itself from, fragmentation can also occur. If a fragmented soul reincarnates, it can create disharmony for the human in the next lifetime, largely because this fragmented soul is 'trapped' in a previous time and place. Soul retrieval, then, is the practice of repairing that energetic tear or damage, thus restoring harmony to the soul, and perhaps the human, too.

Even if we don't always perceive it, we do live in an ever-abundant, ever-regenerating world, and this is also true of our money. We must learn how to tap into the natural energy of ever-growing money and allow it to be true for us, individually, and not just think it works that way for others.

You haven't been put here to merely survive. You have been sent here to thrive, flourish and continually renew and regenerate yourself – start with regenerating your thinking, energy and behaviours and you'll begin to see a new flow of money into your life.

Money-eating entity

Q *My partner and I decided early on in our marriage, probably when the kids arrived, that it worked better for us to pool our money. I've come in and out of part-time work over the past decade as we grew our family, so my work has always been the sporadic income, his the more stable.*

Now, I'm back in the workforce full-time and I'm feeling stifled with the way we have our money set up. My husband isn't controlling, but it certainly feels like I'm hemmed in now – we still pool our money and there's not much of it left over for me, or for fun, or anything other than our family. Family is definitely our focus, but surely now I'm working full-time again, there should be more money than there was before.

I know you're not a financial planner, but I'm really interested in the energy of money and I want to enjoy more of it ... have we got a bad energetic set-up here? What's missing and how could we let more money flow to us?

A I see a clairvoyant image with three different entities, each with their own energy systems and flows – and all three interact and intersect, a bit like a Venn diagram.

71

You are an entity with your own flow of energy and money.

Your partner is his own entity with his own flow of energy and money.

And the family is its own entity with its own flow of energy and money.

What should be separate entities have kind of morphed into one, meaning the energy has also morphed. Energy without boundaries lacks structure and integrity – and it can't hold up the flow you want to move through it. By combining your money flows early on, you've unknowingly created co-dependent flows of energy, both personally and financially. Feeling hemmed in and stifled results from this constriction of the flow of money, of energy, through your relationship, your family and your life. Each entity doesn't have enough flowing of its own accord, and so all three are almost parasitically feeding off one another. Doesn't sound good, right?

All the money coming in is being controlled. Contained. Managed. Even drained by this boundary-less, all-consuming morphed entity. All money that comes in is seen as 'one' and there is no clear boundary or sovereignty around the personal flows of that money and energy. Ultimately it is all one, but we must create clear energetic flows or channels for it to enter, pool and exit in a way that aligns with the individual's flow.

Creating clear and separate flows of money is akin to creating clear and separate flows of energy, thus creating healthy boundaries around each individual and the 'us'. Each entity here – you, your partner and the family – needs separate and clear channels. Creating clear energetic containers for you, your husband and your family, and being very intentional about the way you receive, hold and redirect that flow of energy, will result in a much clearer flow of energy in these areas. Practically speaking, that could mean separate bank accounts for each of the three entities, for example.

Chris adds that when you value yourself and your contribution as much as your partner's, you'll relax into enjoying your money. Receive what you earn for yourself first, then give the surplus to your family. Sacrificial living cannot survive. Adequately providing for yourself will attract more provisions to you, because your intention has changed. You'll signal to the universe that *you* are worthy of receiving. First. Then, your surplus can be shared and enjoyed by others, without co-dependence on one another. You are all sovereign energetic beings in your own right.

. ✦ •

QUESTIONS TO ASK YOURSELF

You might like to meditate on the following questions, use them as journalling prompts, invite your own SST to answer you, or turn an oracle card from The Little Sage Oracle Cards in response.

* What is the source of your money? And the source of that source?
* What does money represent for you? Would it be possible for money to hold a different meaning or story for you?
* What is your relationship to money?
* How does your relationship to money mirror your relationship to energy and flow in your life?
* How could you change the relationship you have with money?

If these questions and answers prompt a deeper enquiry, I've compiled a list of additional resources at helenjacobs. co/ask.

. ✦ •

Family matters

Some say you can't choose your family, but I disagree. At the soul level, you certainly do. So you might want to rethink the way you see them! Seeing our family differently allows us to see ourselves differently. Sharing this sentiment always leads to the next question: Why would soul choose this family? The answer: Soul wants growth and chose the family (and the associated soul agreements, lessons and purpose) accordingly.

Personal growth more often than not comes from the things we *don't* like. To illustrate, let me share the story of my high school geography teacher, whom, for our purposes here, I shall call Mr Smith. We crossed paths in my first year of high school. We didn't get along. I was a pest of a student (to him) and incredibly difficult. I can admit it. I didn't enjoy geography, and I certainly didn't enjoy Mr Smith's classes, so when we finished that year – and I knew I would never take geography again – I celebrated the end of my time with Mr Smith. It was over.

Of course, it was not. Instead, Mr Smith turned up in my senior years as my ancient history teacher. By then, however, I'd mellowed, maybe even matured, and I actually enjoyed both the class and his teaching. I'd go so far as to say we got along that year.

The moral of my story is this: Mr Smith wasn't there to teach me either geography or ancient history. Okay, sure, on one level he was. But, I believe the real reason Mr Smith was there was to teach me about myself – that being a jerk to teachers isn't cool, that learning can be fun and that it's best not to assume someone is a certain way before truly giving them a chance. Mr Smith went on to teach me something far more meaningful than anything I've remembered about either geography or ancient history. And, as much as it pains my thirteen-year-old self to say, he is the teacher I most often refer to in my stories of the good old days. He's now also committed to print.

So it is with families. The overbearing parent. The competitive sister. The absent father figure. However we've labelled them, the lesson for the soul is much deeper. Family. Love 'em or hate 'em, your soul chose them.

Dying to see you

Q *My dad is dying and I don't want to see him. He walked out on us when we were kids. He left Mum to figure it all out with no money, no job – we didn't even have a place to live for a while. He just took off with some other woman and whatever money we had. He clearly didn't care about us. Why should I care about him now? I don't need to hear him beg or say sorry, or maybe he's not going to say any of those things and I'll be even angrier at him. My brother fixed things with Dad years ago. They even became friends. I don't want to forgive him but I might never get this chance again. I'm scared of what I might say to him. What do I do?*

A Ultimately, only you can decide what to do, but I can shed some light on how spirit sees this to help you make your decision.

Believe it or not, your soul chose him as your father. Your soul chose this lesson. Let me be clear: I'm not saying that as a child you willingly agreed to your father's decisions. Those were his and he is responsible for them. But your soul knew that the two of you would teach each other not just about forgiveness but also about unconditional love. (The *how* was open to interpretation and human free will.)

Your father has battled demons his whole life. He felt like a failure. He was raised in a household where there was no love, just abuse. That does not excuse his choices and behaviours, but hopefully puts them into context. Your father is a person, just like anyone else, who has grappled with his life and his circumstances and even his family of origin. For what it's worth, I believe he's realising that now.

His absence also birthed much positivity in your life you're reluctant to credit him with. Without these awful things, you would not have become the strong woman you are. Chris shows me you would never have gone into social work to counsel young kids if it weren't for this formative relationship, or lack thereof, with your father. Despite your challenges with your dad, many people benefit as a result. Lessons lead to purpose.

Your forgiveness is yours alone to explore. Bear in mind, forgiveness is never really about the other person. Forgiveness is not about what happened, or letting him off the hook for his choices and decisions. *Forgiveness is for you.* Forgiveness is about dropping the anger and the hurt, so you're no longer burdened by it. Forgiveness creates space for the new to enter. Peace with your father can be found regardless of whether you go see him or not. Visiting him now doesn't have to be about him, but about you. Don't make your decision from your wound; choose from a desire to free yourself.

Lessons exist in our choices as much as our experiences. Choosing to see your father differently *is* the lesson here. The lesson is in loving anyway. Such love needn't only be directed towards your dad; can you choose to love yourself enough to set yourself free? For two souls who chose to teach each other about unconditional love, it would appear he's holding up his end of the bargain. Could you hold up yours?

Freedom is here to be found, not in the conversation with your father, but in the long-overdue conversation with yourself. Start there.

Family fights

Q *My dad and his sister are in a legal battle with their brother right now over my grandmother's estate. My grandmother owned a large property worth a few million, had multiple investments and established a family business worth millions. My uncle left the business years ago and Dad is now CEO. My grandmother amended her will when my uncle left, bequeathing most of her estate to Dad and my aunt (and their children). Whatever caused the separation, the family never reconciled, so for my uncle to turn up now claiming he's owed all this money is so disgusting. Will he be given this money? Is there anything you can see that I can mention to my dad? He's too generous and I'm worried he's going to let his brother walk all over him.*

A Please don't worry for your dad. This isn't about the money as much as it is about your uncle. He always felt out of place and out of sync with his siblings since early childhood. This dynamic infiltrated the family business many years later. Now, it's turning up in anger about money, but the money is just a trigger. At its core, this is a deep family wound, your uncle believing he's the odd one out and that your grandmother always preferred your father. Whether or not this is true is beside the point; it's how your uncle has always felt and it's blinded him ever since.

Consequently, your father has often felt guilty. He didn't want to outshine his brother; he'd try to deflect his mother's favouritism. He'd attempt to balance the scales for his brother via little things, like giving him his lunch at school or letting him win backyard cricket. What began as a child's innocent desire to make his brother feel better, and lessen the feeling of being put 'above' anyone else, has inadvertently set up this dynamic your dad has with his brother of teaching him that he'd always fix his discomfort. We're now seeing that at a much bigger, more adult – and more financially invested – level.

Karma is playing out here. These family dynamics spill over from previous lifetimes together. In this lifetime, your uncle always felt the score was uneven and has sought to balance it however he could, stemming from their previous life's relationships with each other. Not because the score was uneven, but because he always thought himself lesser than his brother. He craved his mother's love and felt like he never received it (at least in the way he wanted it).

You ask if your uncle will receive money. I suspect he will and this will settle out of court. Fighting the principle of this would end up far more costly, financially and emotionally, than it would for your father to settle this now.

As I've said, it's not about the money. The real healing comes here when your father can release himself from believing his mother favoured him – or that he should feel guilty because of it. His mother took those actions; this is through no fault of your father's. Your dad would give anything to have his brother by his side, to feel like things are right in the world, and that is likely to include settling this matter to, in part, appease your uncle. Your dad's core wound causes him to play peacekeeper for his brother, but it's also contributed to your dad taking such good care of the employees in this business, and of you and your siblings. Fairness and justice are prominent themes throughout your dad's life. He never wanted to outshine his brother; he's often tried to hide from the spotlight as a result.

You may not be entirely satisfied with the resolution here, but it's also not the money-grab you think it is. Money is merely the mirror for the family dynamics beneath the surface.

Love in law

Q *My daughter (Danika) is marrying a woman (Nina) who my husband and I just can't warm to. Maybe it's some sort of culture clash, or maybe Nina is just controlling by nature, but we're not fond of the way she's changing our daughter. Danika thinks we're being judgemental, that we don't want to get to know Nina or that we've got some underlying homophobic issues, which is just plain ridiculous. Danika is shutting us out. Naturally, we're worried. It appears that Nina is manipulating our daughter and turning her against us. Will Danika go ahead and marry Nina? If she does, will it work out? Will we ever have a good relationship with our daughter, and potentially her wife, again?*

A Please trust your daughter. Trust how you've raised her, how you've equipped her for the big, wide world. This is Danika finding her own way. Of course, no parent wants to see their child experience a less than ideal situation. Assuming she is not in immediate danger, these are her choices and decisions. Please trust you've equipped her for this, even if right now it doesn't look like she's prepared.

She is learning here – about her voice and her ability to stand up for herself and her beliefs. Danika's relationship with Nina will greatly shape her, and not necessarily in the way you fear. However, there may be a tough road to watch her walk while she gets there. Love her anyway.

Danika has longed for such a big, all-encompassing love. This is her first deep romantic relationship; she's still coming to understand her own sexuality and power. Danika's confusion will help her learn. Sometimes getting it 'wrong' allows us to see what's 'right'. Mistakes are powerful teachers.

Nina is not the enemy here, even if you perceive her as such. She, too, is learning and growing. Neither woman has experienced healthy intimate relationships before, largely because they have been so cruel to themselves. Both Danika and Nina have struggled to accept and love themselves. Together, their souls unite to explore concepts such as unconditional love, co-dependence to independence and creating clean, loving dynamics. No small feat! That's bound to look a little messy from the outside.

Only Danika and Nina can decide if they will marry. However, Danika will come to see she's worth more than the treatment she's receiving. She'll hold Nina to account, prompting her to grow, change and heal. That transformation can happen in the romantic relationship, or outside of it. Either way, the lesson demands healing will come. Now, you await their choices.

You've raised a strong, capable, brilliant woman who must be trusted to fulfil her own destiny. Trust you've done all you can do, and love her – and Nina – anyway. Danika knows you're there to catch her – give her enough space to fall, but trust she won't need to.

Adoption adaptation

Q *I was adopted by my parents when I was young and I've always known I was adopted. I had a great childhood, a happy home. I've never felt 'less than' or struggled with being adopted (and sometimes I've felt guilty about that, because I know it's not everyone's experience).*

When I was twenty-one, I met my biological mother, Angie. Angie was raised by her mother's friends, a kind of unofficial adoption I think was common back then. Angie struggled with her decision to adopt me out. She felt unequipped to raise me at the time, maybe because of her own upbringing, I'm not sure.

The irony is, I can't have my own children and I'm considering adopting or maybe fostering. I'm single and totally open to how this might happen. Will it? I've heard you talk about repeating pattens, so I'm also naturally curious about the pattern of adoption here. Is there some deeper soul agreement thing going on here?

A Children can come into our lives in any number of ways. Chris suggests you'll enter a partnership with someone who already has children, effectively becoming a step-mother to their children. These children are destined to be raised by you; there is a soulmate agreement in place.

Repeating patterns want to get our attention and your soul is certainly delving into something much deeper here. Your soul is exploring the broad concept and societal definition of parenting, of family, of blood and kin. Society's concepts around the same are also now expanding. Your personal story and unique experience will contribute to the increasing level of consciousness around what parenting really is, beyond biology and the stories attached to adoption, fostering or step-parenting in our society.

Chris says: Tell your story. I clairvoyantly see a book and some sort of support or education for others in store for you. Your soul isn't exploring this for itself; your soul came here to share your story with the world.

As such, you'll become an advocate for children's rights, parents' rights and healing through non-traditional family dynamics. You'll contribute to changing the narrative around parenting and adoption. Please don't feel guilty about your positive adoption experience. Your awareness that not all children start their lives in such positive circumstances will support many. Your soul wants to support children and parents to bring strength and confidence to their stories, situations and the world around them (remembering, of course, there are so many reasons any particular soul would choose to experience this in this lifetime).

This process starts with gently guiding Angie into her own healing. Cycles will often repeat until the lesson is learned. You are not repeating a cycle, but stopping one. And that can ricochet back through your family lineage, both the genetic and soul-family lineage. You're healing across time, space and dimensions. Suffice to say, this is so much bigger than you may think it is. Your impact is so much greater.

When your own children arrive, you will help them find their place in the world. They will understand their relationship with their own biological mother (and I'm not shown details on this situation), but you will help them to find peace within themselves.

Your soul is balancing karma from previous lifetimes here. It is able to heal old wounds and balance old karmic debts. Not only will you find your own peace, but you will ultimately bring peace to thousands of other families simply by offering what you've learned (and how you reached that conclusion) yourself.

.✦ •

QUESTIONS TO ASK YOURSELF

You might like to meditate on the following questions, use them as journalling prompts, invite your own SST to answer you, or turn an oracle card from The Little Sage Oracle Cards in response.

* Why did my soul choose my family of origin?
* Why did my soul choose my (insert a specific family member here)?
* What are the soul agreements and lessons my soul signed on to learn in this family?
* What is my soul's contribution in teaching others in my family?
* What stories about my family of origin and extended family have I absorbed as true for me? Do they really need to be true for me?

If these questions and answers prompt a deeper enquiry, I've compiled a list of additional resources at helenjacobs. co/ask.

.✦ •

Parenthood understood

Following on from a deep dive into delicate family dynamics, this next chapter specifically explores parenthood and all its wondrous teachings and learnings. While family provides the classroom for our soul, it is perhaps the parent–child relationship that presents the deepest, most expansive terrain for our soul.

Parenthood, and its potential, brings with it myriad questions ranging from 'Can I even have kids?' through to questions around the loss of children via miscarriage and termination. Assuming we do then become parents, our focus quickly shifts to how on earth we're meant to raise these little humans while being messy humans ourselves. How we become parents, the bond of parent and child, and whether we even want to become parents – it can be a minefield of questions.

After countless questions concerning parenthood, I've observed there is no one right way to parent. Answers on parenting change as much as the parent I'm talking to, or the various needs of their children. So let me make this clear: I'm no parenting expert and this is not a crash course on becoming the perfect parent. Instead, I share the insights I've received after asking and answering numerous parenting questions for friends.

It all boils down to this: we may not be perfect parents when we're measured by some societal, idealistic version of perfection – but we will always be the perfect parent for our kids, just as your parents were for you. How do we know we're the perfect parents or had the perfect parents for us? Because in choosing our kids and our parents, soul said so.

Infertility

Q *My husband and I have been trying for so long to fall pregnant. Medically, there is no real reason anyone can give us as to why we haven't been able to conceive. We've spent years working on our health, working with different doctors and even alternative health practitioners (which has been interesting to defend to our families and also rather costly).*

We've tried everything and we just can't get anywhere. We had a window of hope last autumn, but we suffered a devastating miscarriage. It's so hard to keep going, to stay positive. But I know my mindset is important so I try not to stay down for too long. What else can we do? Will we ever get our bundle of joy?

A Please don't be so hard on yourself. While it feels like this is the result of something you're doing, or not doing, this is all so much bigger than you, or your partner, or even the doctors and science. That's not to make this feel so unyieldingly out of control, but to hopefully contextualise your situation. There can be peace in the idea that something so much bigger than you is working on this *for* you. It's not against you.

There are many reasons for infertility. Some of them are physical, but they can also be mental, emotional and energetic, too. Modern Western medicine focuses heavily on the science, the biology, but not necessarily the interconnectivity between the mind, body and soul – and yet this is the first place Chris will look when asked to address human issues of 'infertility'. Spirit looks at each of these four layers (the Four Bodies) first, then the science and biology, and, of course, the role of soul is significant, too.

Human bodies are designed to highlight where an individual is in – or out of – alignment with their soul's path and purpose. An issue of infertility, then, can simply be the body signalling something else is out of alignment – not just the body, but perhaps the mind or soul. You've been working to bring balance to the mind, body and spirit. Please keep going – spirit shows me their symbol for cheering you on (I literally clairvoyantly see a group of spirit guides, if you can imagine them, dressed in cheerleading gear, flouncing pom-poms and doing high kicks. Go Y-O-U!).

These cheerleaders now want to show you a bigger gameplay. There's more to this than your desire alone.

Desire is part of the process, just as biology and science are part of the process. But, to spirit, this is an incomplete equation. Fertility is often only thought of as the union of two – of sperm and egg, of partners – but it is actually the union of three. For physical life to be conceived, there must also be agreement from the soul of the baby itself. It has a say, a rather influential say at that, as to when it comes into physical form, when its life will begin. Its soul has great bearing on this equation that science alone cannot solve.

As such, what we see as a fertility issue, spirit sees as a soul agreement issue (even if this isn't covered in your medical consults!).

Each and every person is connected to others by a range of soul agreements or contracts. You might be connected to another soul to help teach them, or to learn (or vice versa). Agreeing to bring life into the world, then, is a very deep soul commitment, and one that is agreed upon not only by the souls of the parent/s but also the unborn child.

Of course, every parenting relationship is different and there are many, many forms of partnership and parenting; these allow for many, many lessons for the incoming child – in fact, for all involved in the soul agreement.

You are already a mother; please see yourself as such. Your unborn children do, and they are already working with your soul to teach you this important lesson. Once learned, you'll be in an even better place to parent the children who will arrive – and, in this instance, I am indeed shown they will arrive.

Connect with the soul of your unborn baby and ask them what they need. To do this, try sitting in deep meditation and call in their soul (or work with a trusted guide or practitioner who can assist you with this). As you connect with your unborn baby in this way, get to know them. Ask them what they need to help prepare for their arrival; their answer may just surprise you. Once you know this, the focus for you will shift. This is not a medical issue in this case, but a soul agreement issue.

Intuitive kids

Q *My eight-year-old daughter, Layla, has mentioned she's seeing and sensing things (spirits?), especially when falling asleep. She says she sees angels and fairies, that plants talk to her and she can relay how her friends at school are having a harder time at home, or what it feels like to be bullied. Layla is sharing this with her classmates, but they're making fun of her. They don't understand what she's seeing and feeling, because they can't see it, so they believe she must be lying and making it up. How do I help her? How do I support her to be open but also try to protect her from other kids who don't understand and are now starting to pigeonhole her as the odd one out?*

A Thank you for seeing your daughter and honouring who she is. Asking these questions, wanting to protect her, shows you are already supporting her, showing her a new way. And this is so different from how you were raised, so you're learning, too. But you needn't protect her unnecessarily as her soul has chosen this exploration.

Layla is incredibly empathetic. This isn't just sympathetic, or emotionally empathetic, but *energetically* empathetic. She can feel, sense and easily internalise others' energy, which can be overwhelming for an eight-year-old (and most adults, too). To help Layla process all that energy, ensure she has an outlet for grounding energy. Teach her how to protect herself energetically so she isn't overwhelmed by other people's energy, which may not always be positive.

Such protection can include:

- visualising white light as a bubble around her to ground and protect her energy

- visualising roots growing out of her feet deep into the earth that can carry away unwanted energy at her command, thus keeping her safely connected to the earth

- a visit to a local crystal shop to select the right crystals to ground and protect her energy; if she isn't intuitively drawn to any, choose smoky quartz, amethyst or clear quartz (she can carry them in her pocket to school)

- saltwater sprays, salt lamps or bowls of salt in and around the home (salt is a wonderful neutraliser of energy and particularly grounding)

- prayer.

Work with whatever Layla is drawn to (because kids, like the rest of us, can be picky about this).

As Layla is already mentioning angels, she may want to call on Archangel Michael to protect her. If she can hear angels, encourage Layla to start a dialogue with them just as she would with anyone else. She can ask questions of them, task them to help protect her energy and request they help her regulate what she's seeing and sensing. At bedtime, Layla can ask these beings to fill her room with white light and protect her in her sleep, so when she moves into the astral planes she's not going to be accosted by additional energies.

Remind her she's in charge. Just because she can access these realms doesn't mean she has to. She gets to say whose energy she wants to interact with, or whose energy gets to come into her energetic field. Knowing how to voice herself and her desires, not just of the physical world but of the spiritual too, may indeed be a life-long lesson for Layla.

Socially, kids are always going to have to find their way in the world, and this topic is as good as any for her to figure out who she is and what she stands for. The more you normalise this for her, the more she will feel like she's not the odd one out. She may also play a role in teaching other kids how to treat her; she needn't back down to make them more comfortable.

Don't forget, Layla has signed on for this, so her soul is interested in learning and finding this out – and choosing how she might like to share this with the rest of the world.

Impacting kids

Q *My partner and I are separating and I'm worried about the impact on our kids (we have two kids: Mia is six and Isaac is four). My partner occasionally abuses drugs and alcohol. He doesn't always make the best parenting choices, especially after a big weekend. He'd never do drugs in their presence, he's not harmful to the kids, but he's lazy. The kids would live on junk food and TV and never go to school if it were up to him. Now we're separating, I worry about what life might look like for my kids when they're alone with their dad.*

I'm worried he isn't going to be a great influence on their lives. I also worry this change and upheaval will be too much for them. They now have two homes and two lives with two different sets of rules (and experiences) at each home. They are so little and I can't help feeling like my previous bad choices, and their dad's ongoing ones, are all at their expense. What can I do to help minimise the impact for them? I don't want to be the cause of years' worth of therapy for them later in their lives.

A Mia and Isaac signed on to learn their lessons in this kind of classroom. They may not have signed on for the specifics of this, but certainly the overarching lesson. Their souls knew much of this ahead of time, so it's not a surprise to their souls. That's not to say you're off the hook with parenting, but rather to help ease the worry and burden you unnecessarily carry. Their souls already knew; trust their human selves will catch up. Trust they also chose you to guide them through this.

Model a new way for them. Embarking on a better life for yourself (and them) models how it's done. Let them witness you making tough choices, owning mistakes and living according to improved standards. You're showing them how to do hard things, process big emotions and experience difficult choices and their consequences.

Assuming Mia and Isaac are not at risk in your ex's presence, let them find their way with him. His presence will provide contrast, from which they will grow and develop. Don't underestimate your children's ability to bring healing to your husband. He also signed on for them – there is deep soul healing occurring here. Your kids will 'raise' your husband – they will command he rise to the occasion – but he has to first see all the ways he's letting them down. Without you there to mask it, he will be forced to see it sooner.

Your family continues to learn the lessons you all agreed to at a soul level, just now through a different lens. Same lessons; different classrooms.

Aborting mission

Q *I'm pregnant and I am not sure I want to be. I'm in a fairly new relationship and it's too early to add this into the mix. My partner isn't sure he wants to have kids, let alone if we're meant to have them together. I actually wasn't sure if I'd ever have kids. In my twenties I had two abortions. I was too young. I was not in healthy relationships either time and I was battling with my own demons. I was not prepared for or capable of raising children; I was barely capable of taking care of myself.*

Now, I'm edging closer to forty and this opportunity to become a parent may not come around again for me. I've watched many of my girlfriends struggle to have children, particularly the older they've become, so I'm incredibly torn. I'm not sure what I should do. Do I terminate this pregnancy, or am I actually being given the chance to choose again? Am I meant to be a mother? I just feel so grateful I live somewhere I even have this choice. I don't want to make the wrong one.

A You do indeed have a choice and this choice is yours alone. I cannot make that choice for you and I'm not here to sway you either way. Instead I hope to provide context from spirit to help you in your own decision-making.

You are being handed an opportunity here to do things differently. You're not who you were in your twenties. You are strong, capable, independent, resourceful, loving, nurturing and very clear on who you are and how you see the world. If you choose to proceed with this pregnancy, please know you are ready for this.

Chris shows me that parenting this child would allow the growth you yearn for, perhaps far deeper than through a romantic, intimate relationship. Parenting this child will hold up a mirror you're now ready to look into. The potential relationship with this child will further your growth and what you have to offer this child is what this child is seeking in this lifetime.

You are supported. You have built a strong network of friends around you. You may also see changes in your family dynamics as a result of this, bringing greater healing to relationships with your family of origin. This child brings great healing – it's part of their soul purpose – regardless of whether they make it here physically outside the womb or not. They have already signed on to become a catalyst for change for you, and your partner, too. This soul is a great initiator. They will forever initiate this growth in your life, whether they physically arrive here or not.

You already have an agreement with this soul, just as you

did with the two pregnancies from your twenties. Motherhood doesn't only begin when a child is physically birthed into the world; it begins long before then from spirit's perspective. You have always been a mother – and motherhood is a relationship between parent and child, interacting and inter-relating in a way that both souls grow and mature. You do not necessarily need a physical body for this to happen. In fact, your unborn children have been with you, raising you, healing you since your twenties. They are part of the reason you've been able to move through such challenges and come out the other end. They've never left your side.

Should you decide to terminate this pregnancy, you do not stop being a mother. You won't stop having a soul agreement with this child; you will simply be choosing not to exercise that agreement here in the physical world. And the growth and the lessons will still have been explored, the agreement still held up, albeit played out a little differently. To soul, it's all growth.

Sometimes our soul agreements with other souls provide a much deeper, nuanced lesson. At one level, there is the decision here of what is right for you, this baby and your partner. At another level, the decision provides a gateway into something deeper, an alternative reality, an alternative lesson that lurks below the surface level here. Indeed, a chance to choose again.

You've already learned the lessons and asked the questions about who you are in the world as a single woman who identified as a non-mother. How might this shift if you were to consider yourself differently? And, once considered, how might you then choose again?

From the spirit world, they do not show me guilt, anger or retribution for choosing not to bring in a life – this baby, in this instance, has signed on to play a huge cosmic role in the growth of your soul. Not every soul is committed to having a human life; often there is enough experience for that soul in the brief encounter of early pregnancy. There is growth and experience for souls in all stages of human experience – conception, gestation, birth and physical growth. To the soul, it's all learning and exploration, for all involved. It is the human mind that measures that experience, and time is no match for this depth.

Please consider your partner in this, too. Trust what he says. Yes, it's early days for you both, but this moment in time, regardless of which choice you make, can serve to bring you far closer together should you wish it to, whether in a continued romantic relationship or as co-parents, or even as not. He has a say – but this is your choice.

There is much on offer here for you. You get to choose what you wish to do with it, and how it will shape you moving forward.

.+ •

QUESTIONS TO ASK YOURSELF

You might like to meditate on the following questions, use them as journalling prompts, invite your own SST to answer you, or turn an oracle card from The Little Sage Oracle Cards in response.

* Why did my soul choose my individual parents?
* Why did my soul choose the dynamic between my parents?
* What are the soul agreements and lessons my soul signed on to learn from these parents?
* What is my soul's contribution in teaching my parents?
* Why did my children (past, present or future) choose me?
* What am I teaching my children?
* What are my children teaching me?

If these questions and answers prompt a deeper enquiry, I've compiled a list of additional resources at helenjacobs. co/ask.

.+ •

Relating, dating, soulmating

Throw in some chemistry and a hefty dose of hormones and our intimate, romantic relationships quickly become an intense classroom for our soul's experience. While our human self seeks #relationshipgoals, soul seeks to see itself reflected through deep intimacy and vulnerability with another.

Society sells us a lot of ideas about what a 'perfect relationship' is meant to look like and the norms we're told to subscribe to. But one of my most fascinating observations over thirteen years of clairvoyantly peering into others' relationships (with permission, of course!) is that relationships come in as many shapes and sizes as the individuals within them. I've seen relationships where the partners don't live in the same house – let alone on the same continent! For them, it worked. There are part-time relationships, multiple lovers, no lovers. Marriage and monogamy. Or free rein and free love. Provided we form these relationships out of mutual respect and consent, there really are no limits when it comes to love, just the ones we impose upon ourselves.

No matter the form and shape our relationships take, they are a Petri dish of growth potential. How else do we learn about ourselves, what we want – and do not want – than with another to highlight where we can go deeper, where we can heal and where we can step more fully into our truth and expression. The grit of our encounters teaches us the most about ourselves, both as a messy human and an explorative soul.

When these interpersonal relationships begin to weave in chemistry and sexual energy, the ante is well and truly upped. Many confuse chemistry or even soul-level attraction as a sure sign of a soulmate, our life partner, 'The One'. Let me tell you, that's not how Chris sees things – and it's often a difficult message to relay.

The quality of any relationship is always a by-product and reflection of the people within it. And ultimately (if you'll excuse the upcoming cliche), the most important relationship we will ever have is with ourselves. Want more love? Love yourself more first. Want more pleasure? Yep, give that to yourself first, too. And you want unconditional love? Start with unconditionally loving yourself. It's the basis of all our relationships.

+ ✦ . + • .

Blurred lines

Q *I'm really attracted to my wife's best friend, Paula. She's currently living with us, which is making things a little awkward. My wife and I have an open relationship. We are free to explore extra-marital relationships with people we don't already personally know or who aren't known to the marriage. So, Paula is different and crosses a boundary we had agreed upon, one that has worked for us for many years. Extra-marital relationships tend to be purely physical; we don't enter into deeper, more meaningful relationships with others. We save that for our marriage.*

I haven't yet broached this with Paula, although she is aware of the arrangement my wife and I have. I believe Paula feels similarly and it becomes messy because we have a shared history as friends. A deeper friendship already exists, both for Paula and myself and for my wife and Paula. There is already an intimacy with Paula that, if we were to become physical, would breach the level of trust within my marriage. Paula and I have not crossed any lines – I haven't even mentioned my feelings to her – and I have always honoured the agreements my wife and I have in place in our partnership. It's what makes it, and us, work. So, my question is, how can I broach this with my wife in a way that won't take our existing relationship agreement somewhere we can't return from. Should I pursue something with Paula?

+⁺ ₊ +˙ ˙

A Honest communication is the very foundation of your marriage. Start there. Your marriage flourishes because you and your wife respect one another and honour the boundaries of your relationship as well as honour each other as individuals. You've developed strong communication styles: you are both willing to listen and truly hear the other and offer unconditional love. Your open relationship works because of this foundation – so trust it here, as well.

I won't pretend to tell you what to do, or how your wife will respond. Instead, I'll share how spirit sees this energy dynamic and its implication, so you have more information to make your own choices and decisions.

Paula has been sent as a messenger of sorts, a mirror highlighting to you a deeper desire and longing in your life or relationship. She speaks to the part of you that is looking for intimacy with someone you are deeply connected to, beyond a physical or sexual chemistry and connection. The yearning for both. Naturally, the curiosity becomes whether you need to pursue this with Paula – but spirit prompts a little deeper.

Let this mirror reflect to you *what* you really want, not necessarily *who*.

Self-enquiry as to why you're drawn to Paula may help you determine what you really want in your relationship/s and/or marriage next. Knowing this will help you pursue whomever you wish to pursue. Your next steps come from understanding yourself. But beware, there is no guarantee who you choose to pursue will also want to pursue you. That is not the goal; you cannot control the outcome by manipulating the situation.

Your marriage already defies what is comfortable for many. You are not looking for what is acceptable for others, but you are constantly working with each other to determine what is, or isn't, acceptable for the union between you and your wife. When you know what you desire, bring that desire to your wife, first. With clearer boundaries, you can then decide if you feel comfortable engaging in a relationship with Paula (assuming, of course, she is willing to go there, too).

Life's challenges often trigger within us the things we need to see, face and heal within ourselves. You can always view Paula as one such mirror. What does she highlight to you? What do you want more of? Less of? How can you address that within yourself, first? And how can you best express your own needs and desires, to yourself, your wife and the world around you?

Paula may simply be pointing you back into an even deeper relationship with your wife.

Empty sex

Q *I've been hooking up with people using dating apps for about two years now. It's been a wild and crazy ride. Literally. I've had periods of no sex at all and then other times, like now, I'm having loads of it with loads of different people. The thing is, it doesn't matter how much of it I am or am not having, it all just feels a bit empty. Like the sex can be great and I still feel shitty. And the sex can be non-existent, and I still feel just as shitty. Isn't sex meant to be this amazing connecter? I don't want the boredom of a long-term physical partner (been there, done that) but the idea of sleeping around isn't really hitting the spot anymore. Am I destined for a life of self-pleasure, or celibacy? Or am I going to find the right person or people who'll get what I'm about and give me what I need?*

A Spirit views sex so very differently from how we view, and experience, sex. Sex isn't purely physical, but a beautiful energetic exchange, the meeting and merging of two life forces, two spirits and two souls. Sex has the potential to harness Big Bang kind of energy – and I don't mean the kind of Big Bang you're expecting!

Let me explain this Big Bang of energy. After all, you are energy. Your partner is energy. Imagine a bubble, a force field, around your body and your partner's body. Consider how those force fields might move and morph when those physical bodies meet, engage, penetrate. In any interpersonal interaction, when two energy fields come together, energy is exchanged. During sex, they aren't just exchanged, they become deeply enmeshed, entwined, joined. Suddenly it's not just a potential partner's emotional baggage we need to consider – it's also their *energetic* baggage. Sex, then, is not just a physical connection, but also mental, emotional *and* energetic.

So, you're now merging and morphing energy fields ... but what's in them? Individual energy fields contain all the secrets of your thoughts, feelings, experiences and behaviours – an energetic imprint of everything you're holding in your life. Not everyone is consciously aware of their energy or actively working to clear it, so engaging in sex is a literal imprinting of someone else's energy field with your energy – and yours with theirs. Without energetic protection or subsequent energy clearing, you take on your partner's energy (and energetic history) during sex. Way more than you bargained for, right?

Accumulating in your energy field right now, then, is the build-up of all that energy – and the accumulation from other people's fields, too. Every interaction, sexual or otherwise, is imprinted in your field. When old, stagnant energy hangs in your energy field too long, it can leave you feeling off-centre, empty or worse.

And, we've arrived at my point: it may not be the sex itself leaving you empty, but the accumulated energy you unwittingly have swimming in your energy field, wreaking havoc in your life. Time for an energetic clear out (try cord cutting, chakra balancing and aura cleansing).

Aura cleansing is a simple practice of clearing your aura, the energy field that sits around your physical body, somewhat like a bubble. You can visualise white light acting like a horizontal scanner, running from the area just above your head and scanning vertically, until it reaches the floor. Cleansing your aura removes unwanted psychic debris from your energy field. Spritzing your body with essential oils and specifically designed sprays may also help clear your aura.

Let's take another tack, now. Perhaps it's not the sex you're bored with at all. Feelings always point us deeper. Where else are you bored, frustrated and empty? Are you seeking answers in the wrong places (and people)? Resolving your boredom, frustration and emptiness negates the need to look outside yourself to fill that need.

All of this and I haven't even mentioned the soul level yet! Regardless of whether you're engaging with 'The One' or just the one to teach you what you need in that moment, every partner offers you a lesson. Thus far, all lessons may simply point to you addressing the feelings of emptiness.

As for a life of self-pleasure or celibacy – well, that's for you to decide. The pressure needn't be on sex to be the answer. Self-pleasure is not bad. Celibacy is not bad. Sex is not bad. But the intentions, thoughts, beliefs and demands of any of these sexual experiences (or any other experience for that matter) are what cause the suffering. When the pressure isn't on the sex to fulfil you, the game changes. And you won't need an external reference for your levels of happiness and pleasure.

Your future relationships needn't feel conventional. But make them energetically clean.

Mirror messengers

Q *There's this guy from work, Julian. Can you give me a read on him? I'm married and I'm not looking to have a full-blown affair, but there's something between us. Chemistry. Sparks. Whatever. He's kissed me a couple of times, but nothing more. I don't consider that cause for ruining my marriage. However, we're travelling together for work next month and things could escalate. I never thought I'd ever contemplate an affair, let alone invite one in. I'm worried about my husband finding out. I don't want to hurt him. If he knew about the flirting and a few kisses, he'd think I'm already having an affair. What do I do? Is Julian really my soulmate and am I in a marriage with the wrong person?*

A Chemistry does not a soulmate make! And a soulmate needn't be 'The One' who 'completes you', as Hollywood may have you believe. But you can bet a soulmate will hold you to account to the lessons you're here to explore. Chemistry and soulmates are two separate concepts and experiences – and lead to two very different outcomes. Before you ride off with Julian, let's break this down.

Let's look at the role Julian plays. Chris calls him a 'mirror messenger'. Such messengers point us deeper into parts of ourselves we haven't explored, or didn't even know existed. What does Julian represent to you? What feelings and desires does he unearth inside you? These feelings – and where they lead you – are the real sign here, not Julian. He's just the messenger. With the message received, you can then decide *where* you want to explore these feelings. Julian? Your husband? Or somewhere else entirely?

You ask if you're in the wrong relationship. Only you can decide that. And, in fairness, your husband should be given a chance to decide that, too. Semantics around an affair aside, there's no full disclosure with your husband. Your actions have already breached his boundaries. Your ego is trying to protect you by controlling and orchestrating the most beneficial outcome for you. Murky energy, unclean lines of communication and blurred trust now need addressing. Your husband may not have an intellectual knowledge of your interactions with Julian, but he may sense the shift in your energy – which is now wreaking havoc on your throat chakra, the energy centre responsible for processing energy around communication, expression, choice and integrity. Speak your truth, even if you fear the outcome. Whatever the message we must express, we can never truly anticipate how others will react. That's for them to decide, not for us to anticipate.

Relationships are a constant negotiation. Each party needs to bring their whole self to the table and allow the other to meet them, teach them or leave them. Expressing your desires, fears and experiences to your husband allows for an honest and open negotiation, for both parties. Don't deny him the opportunity to meet you where you are. He may just surprise you and be willing to entertain these new desires you have unearthed. But, such negotiations cannot be guaranteed. This could go against you. Either way, you will have your answer to that part of your question. But that question needs to be asked of the only person who can give you the answer: your husband.

And so, a picture is painted here: Julian is not the message, but the messenger. Now you have new feelings, urges and desires. What will you do with them? For what it's worth – and without wanting to rock your world anymore than it is already rocking – there may be a third option here. This may not be about Julian, or even your husband (depending on the choices he makes), but instead be about whether or not you are willing to go where the desires lead you, even if it's a pathway not yet clear to you.

Baby daddy

Q *My boyfriend Sam and I have been together for about eight years. I'm ready for marriage and kids but he says he's not ready yet. We're not getting any younger, and I know marriage is important to me, as are kids. I want to experience motherhood. I love Sam so much, but am not convinced we're on the same path, wanting the same things. Does he just need a little more time, or should I be getting out of here?*

+✝.+✝.

A With a gentle, loving nudge, I wonder, was eight years not long enough for Sam to consider this?

Sometimes we simply need to see what someone is really showing us. Sometimes, that *is* the sign. Listen to Sam when he says he's not sure. Even more importantly, listen to what *you* want. Your desires are all the answers you need here, even if they start to lead you somewhere uncertain. But following our intuition and desires isn't for the faint-hearted. And our intuitive nudges become harder to hear when we throw in a genuine love, like that between you and Sam. But does that love give you all you want and need?

Sit long enough in true stillness and connect with your heart, your truth and your deepest desires. Then ask yourself:

'Is this really what I want?' Or, to put it another way, do you want Sam's indecision more than you want to fulfil your own desires?

Clairvoyantly, Chris often shows me relationships as an image of two people sitting opposite one another at a table. In this scenario, you're on one side, Sam on the other. You've arrived here to negotiate. You've stated your case; Sam, his. In any negotiation, the goal is to find a solution both parties are happy with. Both parties state their case, their desires, and listen to the other's, before considering if they're willing to give what they're being asked for. While the aim is a mutually beneficial solution, such negotiations can go one of three ways.

One: you give in and drop your requests. Effectively, in this scenario, Sam's desires matter more and you need to drop your desires, never to speak of them again.

Two: Sam gives in, and your desires matter more. You get married and have children with someone who wasn't committed to this to begin with and hope that it works out well, further down the line.

Three: you meet somewhere in the middle. Such compromise makes sense on smaller things. Can't decide if it's Asian or Mexican for dinner? Compromise with some sort of fusion. What are our plans tonight? You choose dinner; I'll choose the movie. Everyone's happy. But big life commitments, like marriage and children, don't lend themselves so easily to a happy medium. You can't 'kind of' have children.

After eight years, negotiations have stalled. Might Sam change his mind in time? Sure, it's possible, but unlikely. Trust him when he shows you who he is.

The bigger question may be: will you change your mind? Your desires are your biggest clue here. And if they've led you this far, they can lead you to where you need to go to fulfil the desires your soul came here to explore. Children may not be guaranteed, of course, nor that another partner would turn up. However, if I look at the soul agreements here, I see you with children. Following your desires would somehow lead you into the solution you need, even if your head doesn't yet understand the how. Be willing to follow your heart, your yearning and ultimately your soul's desire – without a guarantee that you'll get it in the end.

Your soul was mated with Sam's not necessarily for marriage and children, but to help you realise how important they are to you. His greatest gift to you is the realisation of who you really are and what you really want. And believing you are worth pursuing what you want.

. + •

QUESTIONS TO ASK YOURSELF

You might like to meditate on the following questions, use them as journalling prompts, invite your own SST to answer you, or turn an oracle card from The Little Sage Oracle Cards in response.

* What lessons am I continually learning in my relationships? Am I ready to graduate from these lessons?
* What rules, conventions or expectations am I living by in my relationships? Do they truly work for me?
* What do I truly long for in my relationships (past, present and future)?
* What do I really wish to express to my partner?
* Complete this sentence: If I didn't have to live up to anyone else's expectations about my relationship, I would really want it to look and feel like

_____.

If these questions and answers prompt a deeper enquiry, I've compiled a list of additional resources at helenjacobs. co/ask.

. + •

The ending, the void and the beginning

Death.

Still reading? Surprising ... because in the Western world we spend an exorbitant amount of time, energy and money avoiding and delaying loss, particularly death and ageing. However, we experience death and loss every day. Day ends. Things break. We lose our way ... or we stumble (or smash) into the bigger losses and endings – like a marriage, a job or indeed the loss of life. When we haven't spent time honouring loss and death as a natural, unavoidable part of life, we seem to struggle with it when it comes. And it always comes.

As I write this, our world is experiencing a global pandemic. There is loss everywhere – of life, jobs, dreams, income, freedom and certainty. Amid this shift, Chris led me to record and air a podcast episode discussing the ending, the void and the beginning. (It was episode 70 of *The Guided Collective* podcast, if you're interested.) In that episode, I share how we move through endings physically, mentally, emotionally and spiritually – and we don't always do that simultaneously. For example, a relationship may physically end but we don't emotionally untangle ourselves until some time later. This staggered ending is certainly true of this pandemic (as is the void and beginning): we are yet to fully realise the impacts born out of this ending.

Our egos don't like the void – it's far too uncertain. Ego doesn't like the unknown, but soul does. We dangle in the void, precariously positioned between our old life and our new. The in-between. To soul, this is fertile ground, allowing us to plant the seeds of our new beginnings, especially if we took the time to grieve and let go in the ending. From here, our seeds can take hold – and if it's not what we planted, life will always bring something else into bloom. On the cycle goes. Death is not the end; it's only the beginning.

If you find yourself in the midst of an ending, or in the void, I'm sorry you're there, but it is only one part of your story. There is much that begins out of an ending.

Job loss

Q *For the first time in my life, I've been made redundant. I did get a severance package, but it wasn't great. What do I do now? The economy isn't doing well, unemployment is high and I'm not sure my industry will pick up again soon. I had a good salary and based my life on it (I have a big mortgage and other debts to repay). Perhaps a blessing, or a curse, but I don't have a partner or children to support – or to support me. Do I just take the first job that comes along to pay the bills, or wait it out for the right role? I also didn't expect the blow to my ego and identity. I've struggled to find work and am feeling incredibly low. I don't want to let myself slip into a depression I can't get out of. What should I do next?*

A Feeling low isn't an ideal feeling, but it's an important one. Grieving this loss is important. Please ensure you have support around you, especially if you're worried about your mental health slipping. Check out the services available to you (many are free), such as Beyond Blue, Lifeline or your GP, and do not feel guilty asking for help. Single and childless does not render you an island undeserving of help. Your previous colleagues can support you, if you let them. Asking for help signals a green light for them to step in; they're awaiting your cue. You're an incredibly strong, independent person, so others often mistakenly assume you have everything under control. They won't know what you need unless you tell them – and give them a chance to feel good in assisting. With some extra time on your hands, there are also many new friends to be made.

According to all the facts and figures, it surely is not the most ideal time to lose a job, but then, when would be? While unemployment numbers are high, and there is a lot of fear in the market and in the world 'out there', remember that what is happening 'out there' needn't be your personal experience 'in here'. Focus on who and what is in your control – *you*.

Bearing in mind I'm not a financial advisor and I have not snuck access to your bank accounts (promise!), I can only share Chris's perspective. First, Chris wants you to know you're being taken care of; this is actually working *for* you. The severance package is enough to support you right now (albeit at a reduced budget). Chris also suggests in this current market many institutions are willing to revisit debts and arrange alternative payment options. Worth looking into. You've also been smart with your money to date and can juggle things around to lengthen your runway. These tweaks should bring a little security to your mind, and a reprieve for your nervous system.

But this isn't just about your finances. Nor is this the loss of *everything*. It's just the beginning of something not yet entirely known. Grieve. Farewell the job and the old life, even the identity you once knew. Send it off in style!

Your real job now, in the extra time made available to you, becomes an inside job. Commit to shifting your old identity and opening up to what else is possible for you. Chris calls this your course-correction. A new life awaits – and it could never have reached you while you were so tightly wound up in that job.

Sit in the unknown a while. Set new intentions. Course-correct. Dream and desire something new. Perhaps there is even time now to explore what that might be, and who you might be. Consider an opportunity you wouldn't have taken while you were working those long hours and so committed to the job and career before you.

Inner transformation draws the new beginning to you. My prediction is a whole new career, one that allows you to go out on your own. Employment is often seen as the financial holy grail of security, but the best financial guarantee is backing yourself. Within six months, I predict you will have sold your house, have extra money in the bank, be in a new location (I see water) and be working with far more freedom and flexibility than you ever dreamed possible. A dream not possible to dream where you were before.

Divorce

Q *I'm in the middle of a messy divorce and my ex (Fillipe) is being a nightmare. We have three children together and I forwent a career to be the primary carer. Consequently, I have no real employment experience (other than the little admin I used to do in his business), no savings and no credit history and now have to not only fend for myself, but also for my three children. Fillipe's avoiding paying child support and doesn't want to provide for me and the kids. I have a good legal team, but I don't have much fight left in me for this. Beyond the messy mediation, the hardest part is the loss of our family, my relationship and the life I thought we'd build together. Fillipe already has another girlfriend, who I suspect he was with before we separated. How do I pull myself together? How do I rebuild and take care of the kids and provide everything for them?*

A Please take all the time you need to grieve the end of your world, as you knew it. Grieve the loss of your solid foundation. Rage. Feel it all. We don't always want to feel these feelings, but they need to be felt as they make their way out. Once cleared, you'll be best placed to rebuild.

From what you've described, you were already doing much of this on your own. As the primary carer for your children, you've long carried much of this load, perhaps already behaving akin to a single parent, anyway. On the parenting front, you are capable and ready for this – although I don't believe you will need to do it all on your own. Call in support. Many people want to help – other school mothers, your family and new supports you haven't even met yet. They're coming; call them in.

Although you've relied on Fillipe as the main breadwinner, you are also hugely capable of fending for yourself. Uncertainty and sudden circumstantial change quite naturally shake you. This significant shift in your financial position is indeed prompting you to consider a life you had never entertained before. You may not need someone, or something, else to take care of you – but I can see you will soon begin demanding more for yourself, your life and your kids. You are wildly capable; this situation will teach you this.

Chris shows me that from early childhood you believed yourself incapable, that others were better placed to take care of you and that it was ultimately safer to believe others were responsible for your security, whether physical, mental, emotional or financial. This has caused all kinds of energetic entanglement, which is now unravelling. You will never give your power away again.

Support your base chakra during this period. This is the energy centre at the base of the spine, processing energy associated with your thoughts, beliefs, experiences and actions around safety and security – and this is greatly affected for you right now. Try chakra-balancing meditation, reiki, yoga or using crystals like red jasper, which aligns with the base chakra. Moreover, work on your beliefs and mindset around your safety and security.

This ending may happen in stages as it occurs across your Four Bodies:

- **Physically**, you've parted ways with your ex, but there is still a separation of the remainder of your physical life together – the house, the money, even custody of the children. This process will take time, but, as you say yourself, you have a great legal team on board to support you with this. Please find the fight to honour your needs. Fillipe is betting you won't.

- **Mentally**, you'll need to process all that's happened (and you can seek professional support for help with this). You'll rework your beliefs, understanding that how you saw yourself and the world led you into that marriage to begin with, so you could learn what is needed – and rewire that belief system, so you can draw new relationships to you in the future more aligned with your truth and power.

- **Emotional** disentanglement can be the longest to move through. Grief moves in funny ways, and can often surprise us many months or even years down the track. Soul sees it all as data. Showing your emotions to your kids models for them how to move through their own big emotions here. They're watching and learning. They signed on for this.

- **Energetically**, or spiritually, this is the ending and separation of two entwined souls, who made vows and promises, at an energetic (and soul) level, too. Try cutting energy cords to Fillipe (there's a guided meditation on my website) to free you from the energetic field of your husband. You may even want to explore the soul agreements you and Fillipe had through past-life regression or a reading of your Akashic Records (see next page). For what it's worth, I believe your souls agreed to learn about true empowerment, which Fillipe is now ensuring you learn.

When you have honoured your ending across all four layers and allowed yourself to be in the void where you don't yet know exactly what is about to begin, then you can truly begin anew.

The **Akashic Records** are an energetic imprint of thoughts, actions, beliefs and intentions of every soul recorded over time. These are not a physical record but an energetic one, so 'reading' them requires some psychic sight. Accessing your own Akashic Record can help you understand your unique soul blueprint, past lives, and lessons and purpose for this lifetime (and others).

Death

Q *I'm really struggling since my son Mason died. He was twenty-one when he died in a motorcycle accident. We still don't really know what happened that night, the police can't really tell us, just that it was some sort of accident. I never thought I'd be here longer than him. He was so full of life. Such a character. Does he know how much we love him? Can he still hear me? Is he okay? I guess I just want him to know how much we all miss him, every single day. I want to reach him somehow.*

A Death often leaves those behind with the feeling they cannot connect with their loved ones, but this is not the case. The language has just changed. Where we come from and where we return to is a world of the non-physical, so when someone dies physically, they simply return to the world of the non-physical. The challenge for us in the physical world is to open to our non-physical senses. Love is a non-physical language, a communication tool we are all familiar with, regardless of whether we are physical or non-physical. You cannot see love; you *feel* it. You can feel it whether your loved one is physically present or not.

So is the case with death.

Our loved ones in the non-physical world are still with us. Mason is still with you, in spirit. Spirit tries to communicate with us beyond the language of love, but it takes a lot for them to lower their vibrations to match the vibration that most people on earth have been operating at. For many people it's difficult to raise their vibration to match the spirit world, especially when they're experiencing grief. (Chris says that our collective ability to raise our overall vibration is rapidly increasing, however.)

When you think of your deceased loved ones, they know. When you talk about them, they know. They do not judge these thoughts and conversations as they may have in life; they move beyond ego and judgement in the non-physical world. Instead, they are aware of your love for them, the regrets, the things left unsaid and all the pain you're feeling now in their absence. For all the love, hope and loss you're feeling, too.

When someone moves to the other side, they move through a process of review. This process may begin either in the lead up to death, or following, particularly if death has been sudden. The world of spirit does not have clocks or physical time as we do here, so what we may perceive as a lengthy review may indeed be relatively fast for spirit. Such a review is somewhat similar to a workplace performance review. The soul 'meets' with its Spiritual Support Team, reviewing the soul's blueprint and how the soul chose to enact the areas of exploration. This review occurs without judgement (because judgement does not exist in the non-physical spirit world) to consider how the soul fared with their lessons and sharing their purpose and gifts with the world. Areas that need further explanation, or a balancing of lessons, can be held over for exploration in another lifetime, hence the idea of karma.

> Think of your **soul blueprint** not as a physical document, but as an energetic imprint containing the agreements and areas for exploration your soul committed to in this lifetime.

Just as the soul moves through review, so, too, does the spirit. In this process, the spirit – the higher consciousness attached to just this lifetime, as opposed to the soul, which is attached across many lifetimes – comes to see all of human life so differently from how it is experienced in the physical world. However, just because someone leaves their physical body and communicates to us from the world of spirit, it doesn't automatically mean they take on a more 'god-like' awareness. The spirit can continue a process of review and advancement outside of the physical body and life. For this reason, I caution people not to blindly follow the guidance of a loved one in spirit; take their advice through your own intuitive lens, just as you would in life.

That said, as the spirit moves through further growth unattached to human ego and judgement, a higher perspective can be reached. This perspective, no longer tainted by ego or attachment, is higher than what was ever perceived or experienced in human form. Peace can be made; a bigger picture can be gleaned. Attachment to stories, situations and scenarios drops away. Only love remains.

Mortality

Q *I've just been diagnosed with terminal cancer. My doctors say I may have only a few months remaining, but they don't really know. Maybe my time will come sooner. I don't see anyone benefiting if this is drawn out. I'm a single mum of three children, young adults now. They're old enough that I can leave knowing I've done my job well, but young enough that I know there's still so much for me to miss out on. I'm going to miss them falling in love, getting married and having babies of their own. I won't get to see – or enjoy – who they become.*

I'm struggling to find peace with my imminent departure. Where do we go? What is death like? Will I be alone? And do I want to be? How do I farewell my children? I am in some pain; it's mostly managed, but I've wondered about euthanasia. Is it wrong? How am I supposed to face the end?

A Perhaps the only thing we know for certain is that death will one day be upon us. Nevertheless, we can still be surprised by its arrival. We may try to delay it, fight it, resist it, but rarely do we welcome it in.

From the perspective of our spirit guides, death is merely a transition. We move from one dimension to another, from the physical to the non-physical. There is no pain for the soul, no trauma per se, unless we fight it hard. (There are times when death can result from a sudden impact, such as a car accident, and there is a shock to the soul. I've worked with recently deceased spirits who can't quite figure out that they have departed the physical world, for example.) Your soul already knows how to move through this transition. Your job, at the human level, becomes surrendering and releasing to allow the process to gently unfold. Just like in birth, the trick is to surrender to the unknown.

While I can't speak to the euthanasia laws of where you may reside, and nor do I wish to influence that personal choice for you, I can share that from spirit's perspective there can be peace and dignity in choosing that option. All choices and decisions incur karma, but there is a world of difference between avoiding our lessons and pain, and lovingly surrendering to them.

We never truly do death alone. It's your choice as to whether you want loved ones physically present. I believe you will have time to call upon them, to say (and *feel*) your goodbyes, before your moment of transition. You already know how to farewell your children; please know your spirit and soul will indeed be aware of all that is happening at the time of death (should consciousness be lost) even if your physical body is not.

On the other side of the veil, you are likely to be surrounded by many in the spirit world. It is not unusual for loved ones gone before you to gather near you as you begin your transition. They will work with your soul to guide you and light the way. Your own spirit guides will be present, and you can call upon 'specialist guides' to assist you in your transition through prayer in the lead up. It would be their honour to assist you.

Peace fills a room when death arrives. There is a brief moment, a sliver of time suspended, where the veil briefly lifts between two worlds. This is a sensation anyone in the room can perceive. It's palpable. You will become free of your body, a lightness reinstates, and your spirit simply slips across the threshold. As I write this, I clairaudiently hear an angelic choir – a euphony of joy echoing on the other side to mark your arrival home.

Yes, death can indeed be a joyous, miraculous occasion.

From a personal perspective here, if I may (rather than purely a psychic one), being present in the room when a loved one leaves this world has been one of the most transformational moments of my life. I've helped bridge the gap for them, straddling between the physical and non-physical dimensions with them, psychically seeing and energetically perceiving what is occurring on both sides. I've personally witnessed their loved ones in spirit arriving, calling to them and drawing them over with arms wide open. I've seen snippets of their life review, of them pondering what has been and, if they're lucky, of *truly* feeling such immense gratitude for such a life to begin – and end – with.

I have witnessed birth and I have witnessed death – and I see them as one and the same. Both are beautiful, precious and miraculous. You will go out as you came in – forever loved and held in the hearts of many, both in the physical dimension and the world of spirit to which you will return home.

. ✦ ˙

QUESTIONS TO ASK YOURSELF

You might like to meditate on the following questions, use them as journalling prompts, invite your own SST to answer you, or turn an oracle card from The Little Sage Oracle Cards in response.

* How easily do you allow change in your life?
* How could you invite in change, or endings, into your day-to-day life?
* What are some natural transition points in your days, weeks, months and years that would allow you to soften to change and endings?
* How do you feel about: Loss? Endings? Death?
* What expectations do you hold about life? How long should things last? What does it mean when they end?
* What else is possible when something changes?

If these questions and answers prompt a deeper enquiry, I've compiled a list of additional resources at helenjacobs. co/ask.

. ✦ ˙

Healthy Four Bodies

Ever had a niggle that you couldn't quite figure out? Or some unexplained ache or pain that came and went? Or maybe you've experienced far greater health concerns and struggled to reconcile just why they occurred, or where they stemmed from. What if we shifted our thinking from our wellbeing as something to be managed, to something we are in relationship with, where we view it as a litmus test for soul alignment, or as a great revealer of what our soul has come here to learn. Our body always knows.

When it comes to physical and mental health, I've been asked questions aplenty. As I've said to every one of those friends, I don't pretend to have a medical background, nor do I particularly consider myself specialised as a medical intuitive (someone who can psychically see and sense ailments in the body). Where I do consider myself knowledgeable, if you'll indulge me this confidence, is in the realm of energy and mind–body–spirit connection. Chris and the world of spirit always emphasise the connectivity between our physical bodies and our soul path – and this *is* my area of expertise.

I'd hate to think anyone reading this would take these insights in lieu of professional medical advice. It's not my goal to replace medical advice; instead, I wish to support and expand it. Let's look a little broader for our answers and definition of health – what would it look like to be not just physically and mentally well, but also emotionally, energetically and soulfully well?

When we take into account the connections of our physical, mental, emotional and energetic bodies, we don't just want to mask a symptom, but instead look more curiously at what is turning up and run it through not only science, but also our soul's blueprint. Now, if only we could have that included in our medical consults!

Mental health

Q *I've struggled with depression and anxiety for most of my adult life. I find this challenging for obvious reasons, but mainly because I had big dreams for my life. That soul calling you talk of, I'm sure I have it – but I am devastated these dreams may never be realised, which only makes me feel even worse about myself. My meds caused me to gain weight and I have zero motivation to exercise, which doesn't help. My menstrual cycle isn't quite right. It's really painful some months, further affecting my state of mind and mood. Despite the numerous doctors and even alternative health professionals, I can't seem to shake this. There's so much conflicting and confusing information and none of it seems true to me. I just don't believe that I have to put up with this. This isn't a life I want to live. Is there something I'm missing, or something I haven't yet tried that would help?*

A To address your concerns, let's look at all four of your bodies – physical, mental, emotional and energetic. Hopefully looking so broadly will further support what your doctors are working on with you and broaden your scope of investigation. We need to dig a little deeper, connect dots in a different order.

First, Chris is showing me his symbol to relay that your physical body isn't absorbing nutrients in the way it's designed to. No matter how healthily you eat, your body isn't able to take on the nutrients it needs. You're going to so much effort to eat clean but gaining near to nought.

Not only is the balance of nutrients out, so are your hormone levels. Medication has contributed to this over time, so it becomes difficult to tell which cycle kicked off the balance first. Nevertheless, you can work with your health and medical professionals to understand this balance of nutrient absorption and hormone levels and then course-correct. Chris suggests this is also connected with the symptoms of depression and anxiety. All are linked and need to be treated as a whole ecosystem. Attempting to suppress the feelings of depression and anxiety may further imbalance your body.

Second, the physical, anatomical body is one of the most important – and most obvious – sources of guidance. It's more than just a flesh suit! Depression and anxiety, when viewed a little differently, can highlight something deeper to explore in your internal world. Counselling and psychological support may help you reach it, but we also need to understand the role the energetics play here. This cannot be treated physically or mentally *alone*. There are more bodies to contend with.

Beyond your physical being is your energetic being. Energy moves through energy centres (the most commonly known are the chakras) and is stored, or imprinted, in our energy field (think of it like a kind of bubble of energy encasing our physical body). Every thought, interaction, behaviour and action impacts our energy field; it's in a constant state of flux. So, consider for a moment how much is stored there that you've been lugging around with you and had no idea about!

Awareness of our energy, and allowing it to move freely and easily through our system and field, brings us into a state of harmony, or what people often call a state of 'flow'. When the energy field is damaged, or the energy itself is stagnant or storing old hurts and wounds, we can feel our balance leave. We no longer feel in flow; rather, we feel stuck, stagnant and, at times, depressed and anxious.

When our energy is out of balance, it will eventually show up in our physical body (as well as our emotional and mental bodies, too). Our physical body responds to what's in our energy, and sends signals, like the symptoms you're experiencing, to get our attention and encourage us to address the issues. Instead, we mask them, attempting to cancel the symptoms, rather than trace them deeper and treat them at the root cause.

Time for some inner reflection. When did your depression and anxiety begin? What was going on in your life at the time?

What energy would have been stored in your system – and for how long?

Alongside your medical professionals, consider working with a trusted energy practitioner, like a reiki master or bodyworker, too. When I'm selecting a new healer or practitioner, I'm definitely looking for a trusted recommendation, but then I'll also intuitively check my choice, or ask my SST for a green light to work with that provider. Broaden your physical support team and work to remove, clear or unblock energy (typically from stressful or traumatic moments in our life). By doing this we can achieve a knock-on effect across the physical, mental and emotional bodies. Do this simultaneously as you work with the physical, mental and emotional layers, too.

Depending on the results of this work, you might find it could even be an issue that originated not just in this lifetime, but in a previous one. This would then require soul-level healing – for example, through soul retrieval or past-life exploration and healing. But let's address this lifetime first!

Sick kids

Q *My son was diagnosed with cancer when he was just two years old. We've been lucky and received marvellous care and I'm pleased to say my son has been in remission now for a few years. My question is really why. He was so young. He hadn't lived enough life to cause the cancer. Why would children be born into this world to experience such health issues so early in their lives? How do you explain this, when it can't simply be the build-up of energy?*

A I'm so pleased to hear your son is in remission and enjoying his life beyond his cancer experience. No doubt, seeing our children suffer raises so many questions. But there are so many reasons for ill health, and not all of them follow the logical, scientific route we're familiar with.

Sometimes our physical bodies show disease and illness as a result of our lifestyle. For example, we know smoking can lead to lung disease. But in your son's case, we can't fathom how lifestyle choices contributed to cancer, or illness in general; his youth seems to preclude lifestyle as a contributing factor. Basic cause and effect – like our body gains weight when we haven't exercised or are eating poorly – can be ruled out here in your son's case. Also ruling out genetic predisposition, we need to explore answers beyond the physical. And, not surprisingly, I am going to go to the soul level.

Souls *choose* to incarnate to experience such a thing; our human minds, of course, have a very hard time justifying and reconciling that. For your son, his soul may have chosen to experience illness (if not the particular type of cancer he experienced), not because of the illness itself, but because of the soul classroom it created. He was not the only student in this classroom – consider what all other family members and health professionals (and now even people reading this book) may learn. That's a significant butterfly effect from one soul's choices.

So, why on earth choose this?

Karma can accumulate lifetime to lifetime. I think of this in terms of lessons not yet fully learned, or choices made or avoided in a previous lifetime. (It all catches up with us, eventually.) Perhaps your son's soul experienced illness in another lifetime – but didn't beat it, or chose euthanasia or some alternative ending. Incarnating into this life, for example, his soul may have wished to experience *overcoming* illness, as he has now done.

What a soul explores in one lifetime may later also be explored in a subsequent lifetime, but perhaps from a different viewpoint. For example, if your son's soul has a purpose linked with healing, his soul might choose one lifetime as a doctor, one as a patient, one as an anti-vaxxer, one as a herbalist and so on. Same theme, different classrooms. In all of these hypothetical scenarios, the soul can go quite deep into the exploration of health, the human body, the mind–body–spirit connection, our connection with our natural world and so on. Choices made by soul prior to incarnation can surprise and challenge us – if we ever even become privy to them in human form at all!

And perhaps we're still looking at it back-to-front. What if your son didn't actually choose to experience *illness*, but his soul desired true *health*, or a true embodiment into a physical form?

Your son is still quite young. We are yet to see how this pivotal early experience in his life is going to influence his life's path. He may never have become who he came here to be without this formative beginning.

Clearly, I cannot categorically tell you why your son got cancer, nor, in this case, can science. But in the absence of science, I believe it points us towards something bigger, some bigger consideration that is not for the human mind to comprehend. And, it may not actually matter – to your son's soul, it's all perfect the way it is.

Unanswerable ailments

Q *I'm a self-confessed health nut. I grew up in a house where health and wellbeing were ingrained in us. I've lived so rigidly taking care of my health that I thought it would make me immune, literally and figuratively. Turns out that didn't work. I keep getting this pain in my left jaw, like a shooting pain. Sometimes I get unexplained pains in my stomach, too, which I don't think are related. But I notice it's just these kind of phantom pains that never show anything on scans or tests. Doctors aren't sure what's happening. On paper, I really am in perfect health, but I just feel like there's something else going on. How could I be so healthy and still have these weird unexplainable pains?*

A Feeling like you're doing all the right things, but still falling short can be awfully demoralising. And, you're right, you are in good health. This suggests to me it isn't a health issue, per se, not in the traditional sense of modern medicine. Instead, we need to look at what these phantom pains are drawing your attention to.

Each location on our body has a deeper, symbolic meaning. Louise Hay compiled a brilliant resource on this front, and includes a great directory of ailments and their deeper meanings in her book *You Can Heal Your Life*. However, it's our individual interpretation of the symbolism that matters, so please use Louise's book (or others) as a reference, but be guided by your own intuition. (I often have a different interpretation for the ailments Louise suggests, for example.)

Many times, I've seen the jaw represent our ability to clench too tightly – to ideas, to life, to situations. The jaw can flare up when we have issues around our flexibility, our openness to life and our ability or willingness to receive the full richness and zest of life. When your jaw pain next flares, pay attention to what else is going on in your life and consider what your body is trying to tell you about it.

The stomach represents our ability to digest – not just food, but ideas, change, situations and more. How well do you assimilate new beginnings and changes in your routine (flexibility is also linked to the jaw) or your life in general? Again, notice any correlation between the timing of the pain and what else is going on in your life: therein lies your clue.

What appears to be unrelated, I actually see as one and the same. Both the jaw and the stomach are part of the same digestive system, highlighting the process you take from opening wide to receive richness and nourishment (in all its forms) into your life, through to how you process, digest and assimilate that nourishment, and even how you separate and eliminate the old and unwanted.

Your body is asking you to relax your grip, to be more flexible in your thinking about life and to allow more of it to pass through you. And, here's the kicker: I think the stringency of your health is part of the very thing to relax your grip on. Food for thought.

With all things, our intention is important. You can be healthy, but with an off-centre intention. To be so fixated and obsessive with health is just a tricked-up form of control, which can influence the sacral chakra (also linked with lower digestion). There's a whole world of difference between the person who eats well as a form of deep self-love, versus the person who eats well to control and influence their size and shape, born out of a low sense of self-love. Intention counts.

. ✦ ˙

QUESTIONS TO ASK YOURSELF

You might like to meditate on the following questions, use them as journalling prompts, invite your own SST to answer you, or turn an oracle card from The Little Sage Oracle Cards in response.

* What is the current state of each of my Four Bodies?
* What does my physical health want me to know?
* What does my mental health want me to know?
* What does my emotional health want me to know?
* What does my energetic health want me to know?
* What do I need to clear, heal, restore or manifest in my physical, mental, emotional or energetic bodies?

If these questions and answers prompt a deeper enquiry, I've compiled a list of additional resources at helenjacobs. co/ask.

. ✦ ˙

Friend or foe

Compiling the Q&As for this section on friendship occurred over two sittings. Perhaps not coincidentally, my friends were present for both. First, at a writing retreat a circle of friends planned long before I had even signed a book deal – but one I'd agreed to attend anyway. Life already knew.

The second was while I was out writing. I'd driven all over Brisbane, waiting to be intuitively *called* to the best writing location for the day (#stuffpsychicsdo). I wound up at a lovely national park, positioned myself in the sun and got to writing. After about an hour or so, two of my dear friends arrived, also to write. I had not physically contacted them, nor they me. We joked we were able to magnetise ourselves to each other when needed.

I once only dreamed of friendships such as this! They're real (if you want them). Fostering and nurturing deep soul friendships is possible, just as you can experience a deep inner knowing you've found your people (or, that they can find you in any location by psychic sense alone!).

As we've already found, relationships are the soul's classroom. Even the perfectly platonic ones. Friendships can also provide deep soul connections – but they are also a breeding ground for a deep sense of loss, confusion and pain. Such is life.

Increasingly, questions from friends have focused on a deepening sense of loneliness and disconnection, a deep yearning to find 'our people'. In an age where we are so digitally connected, we are mourning the loss of true physical and emotional connection.

Friendships – or, often, the absence of them – offer our souls the opportunity to learn a great deal about itself and life. Seeing others helps us see ourselves.

Friend request

Q *I don't think I really belong anywhere. I look on Facebook and Instagram and see all these people hanging out, at parties, on holidays but I don't get invited. I mean, I don't really want to go to those parties and go on extravagant holidays, but I do want to connect with people who get me. I've been going through a huge spiritual shift and want to find people on a similar wavelength. I'm longing for interesting, thought-provoking conversations. I couldn't care less about what I'm wearing, or the latest bar or the coolest new whatever. The It Crowd sucks. Does what I'm looking for even exist? How do I find my people?*

A Ironically, you're not alone in feeling alone. But this may not be any consolation right now. Perceiving and assuming what other people's friendships are like can be disheartening at best, but downright deceptive at worst. Even those who appear to be surrounded by throngs of people can *feel* lonely and disconnected; they may just do a better job pretending or presenting otherwise.

Huge internal changes, like the one you describe you're experiencing, require our outer world to catch up. And it sounds like you're just in the messy middle, in the void, where you're no longer part of the life or social circles of before, but not yet fully arrived in the new life and new friendships awaiting you.

Trust what you desire is your true guidance – you're aware that there are others out there trying to find you, too. But you won't find new people in old places. If you aren't already, start attending events and classes that align with your interests. Join a meditation group or go to a talk on a topic you find interesting. Go where 'your people' will be gathered, either physically or online. Start by following the intuitive nudges you receive – if you've been thinking about trying a new class, or signing on for that new online group, consider this confirmation to follow that lead. Then follow the next lead and the next. There may be some messengers who arrive to introduce you to the friends you're seeking. Each step leads to the next. Follow the breadcrumbs.

Often our disconnect from others stems from a disconnect from ourselves. Your self-discovery expedition is guiding you into a deeper love for yourself. The deeper you go with your relationship with yourself, the deeper you will go with your friendships. Energies have to match. You're now drawing to you people comfortable with themselves – with enough love to offer you, too. Trust your outer world is reorganising itself to reflect the inner world change you've moved through.

Don't forget to let these new friends in when they arrive. Previous hurts and disappointments have a way of precluding future friendships if left unchecked. Continuing to believe you don't belong means you won't. Exercise your choice of which friends, social circles and gatherings will be honoured by your presence. This isn't a one-way street. You cannot force others to accept you, but you can accept yourself, wholeheartedly. With that fierce self-love and self-friendship, you'll realise there is nowhere in this world you do anything but belong.

Bestie break-up

Q *How do you break up with a friend? I'm ready to move on, but my friend's not. I feel awful about it because she doesn't really have too many other people in her life, and she's a bit clingy because of it. She's had a hard life and doesn't trust a lot of people, but sometimes I wonder if she uses that a little bit to keep me here. Argh, I feel so awful even saying that about her. Yet she won't take a hint. I don't know how to tell her I don't want to be her friend anymore. I can't keep pretending to be someone she wants me to be, or who I used to be. I need to move on and I don't know how to tell her.*

+ ⁺ ● + ⁺ ● ●

A You are not responsible for your friend's feelings. You are under no obligation to make things easier or more comfortable for her. You do not need to dampen your desires for someone else. You are, however, responsible for being open and honest, for being clear in your energy, your boundaries and your intentions. Saying one thing but doing the opposite not only creates messy mixed messages but really messy energy exchanges. And you don't want that kind of energy interfering with your field – or your friend's. That's not fair to either of you.

Consider how you might remove yourself from the friendship physically, mentally, emotionally and energetically. For a refresher on these Four Bodies, see page 259. Let's start with the energetic body (my favourite place to start!). Clear your energy centres (chakras), cut psychic cords and strengthen your own internal energetic container. Clear, strong energetic boundaries will reinforce your clear, strong intentions, actions, thoughts and behaviours (and you can take your time to set them, too).

Clearing up your energy automatically has a knock-on effect to the other bodies. Your emotions around this friend and your relationship will pass (but they may need to rise first – prepare yourself!). Old hurts or wounds, from this friendship or others, will need to make their way out through this process. Don't worry if anger, jealousy or resentment (or whatever else) surfaces. Just see it as confirmation this is working. Better out than in.

The mental purge tasks you to reflect on the beliefs you hold around friendships. What are the unspoken (or perhaps even spoken) rules of this or any other friendship? What expectations and stories are you beholden to? How are they preventing you from doing and being what you want and need in this situation? Try writing out all the things you believe about your friend and your friendship and then question each belief. Replace it with something more supportive.

Although this may take some time, it'll be worth it. And it doesn't need to be complete for you to exit the relationship, but its completion will allow you to fully step out of it clearly, across all Four Bodies. Clearing up your insides will help you to speak your truth, voice your desires and action your needs. And, to send her love on your way out.

Two birds, one stone

Q *Is it wrong to be jealous of my former best friends? Ciara and I had been best friends since the start of primary school. She was like a sister to me. We even lived together through uni. In my late twenties I became friends with my colleague Samantha. Inevitably, I introduced Ciara and Samantha. They fell in love and cut me out. They just created this life together overnight and left me out of it. I was devastated and heartbroken. I lost my two best friends in one hit. Before same-sex marriage was legal, they had their own version of a commitment ceremony and I wasn't even invited. Do they ever think of me? Are they sorry for how they treated me?*

A None of your emotions are ever wrong, despite what others may tell you. Emotions are powerful indicators, turning a spotlight on what you need to know or where you need to heal, or indicating decisions requiring attention. Therefore your jealousy is valid, because you feel it. Uncomfortable, yes. Wrong, no. Seems like you stand to learn a lot by asking the jealousy what it wants you to know.

Jealousy can point us towards what we wish we had. Jealousy asks us to believe that what we see others experiencing is possible for us, too. Perhaps you long for a love like theirs? Maybe you desire a deeper friendship than either of them were able to give you? Maybe this runs deeper – it could be a long-held belief you don't belong, or that you're always abandoned by those you love. I suspect this is not the first time jealousy has come up for you. When did you first experience this emotion (or the underlying causes)? Can you heal that?

Energy around this event still needs to be expressed, even if the words remain unsaid. Write your feelings out and burn the paper. Talk to a confidant or therapist. Paint it out. Punch it out on a boxing bag. Howl and rage and cry it out. Stored emotions are never good for us and, while you may be angry and hurt by your former friends, you're only continuing to hurt yourself by hanging on to this. The punishment does not fit the crime (and, frankly, no crime was ever committed – by either party).

Did you grieve? Did you give yourself permission to feel betrayed, angry and hurt – or did you play along like nothing was wrong? Did you deny your feelings and bottle them up? Who was there to catch you? Did you – could you – catch yourself? Could you be the friend you needed? What would it look and feel like to give yourself the things you wanted to receive from Ciara and Samantha? What if you could be kind and nurturing and loving to yourself? How might this shift you out of the hurt and pain and into a new beginning? It's there if you want it, when you're ready.

Viewing this situation from a higher perspective, this friendship experience is asking you to step more fully into *your* truth, into *your* fullness and brilliance, and to love and accept *yourself* – even if you've been telling yourself they didn't. Our human self can see others as the 'bad guys' when really, at the soul level, they have provided us with a great gift. Recognising and acknowledging that gift can take some time, but the gift here is in awakening you to who you really are and what you really want.

Reconsider the meaning you've attached to this event. Is it true? Could there be another meaning? What if they were embarrassed? What if they were so mortified they'd hurt you? What if they have been punishing themselves? While we don't know if that's true or not, simply *entertaining* the idea that the meaning of this event could be different starts to loosen the mind's grip on the narrative in your head. It will eventually set you free.

You ask whether they ever think of you – only they can truly answer that. However, you are such a pivotal part of their story, the reason they came to be. Would it be possible for you to see what a gift you've given your old friends? While it didn't turn out perfectly for you, it was a real life-changing occurrence for them, in which you were pivotal. You are a powerful player in their story, just as they are in yours.

.✦ •

QUESTIONS TO ASK YOURSELF

You might like to meditate on the following questions, use them as journalling prompts, invite your own SST to answer you, or turn an oracle card from The Little Sage Oracle Cards in response.

* What is the soul agreement, lesson or purpose my soul is exploring with my friends?
* What are the expectations I have about my friend-ships? Are they fair?
* What are the expectations my friends have of me? Are they fair?
* If my friendships are mirrors, what are they showing me about myself?
* What kind of friendships do I desire most? Who might I need to become to foster these desires in my friendships?

If these questions and answers prompt a deeper enquiry, I've compiled a list of additional resources at helenjacobs. co/ask.

.✦ •

Spirited spirits

Inevitably, the questions I am most asked pertain to the world of spirit. How do I connect with them? How do I do it? How do *you* do it? And what are they saying? Much of this I addressed in my first book, *You Already Know*. For now, then, I've gathered a collection of questions that didn't really fall into that book, questions of a far bigger, broader predilection enquiring into the role of spirit, soul, twin flames, fate and free will. Herein lies spirit's take on themselves.

I wasn't joking in the introduction when I said that asking questions leads to several more begging to be asked. So it has been with my spiritual Q&A over the years. Despite asking thousands of questions (nay, countless questions!) of the spirit world for myself – and on behalf of my friends – for well over a decade, I still haven't reached a definitive end. More like I've begun an exploration of a bottomless pit (or, perhaps more accurately, an expansive cosmos). I may never return again!

One thing's for sure: spirit hasn't told us all there is to know (at a mental level) about our world, our universe and how this crazy thing called life really works. As we move through a collective increase in our frequency, we are being given the opportunity to remember much more than we've known before – yet there is still so much shrouded from us here. All in divine timing, as we are ready to receive it. Typically, when I'm not going to be given an answer, I see a clairvoyant picture of someone smirking, arms folded across their chest, simply shrugging at me. Humph.

Putting aside what spirit won't yet tell us, they are definitely here to help us in our soulful quest to remember our own spirituality and to reconnect to our own truths and universal truths. And we each must take that journey on our own. The questions and answers here may just help unlock something in you to begin – or recommence, or even deepen – that spiritual journey.

Message mule

Q *Lately, I've been picking up on people's energy. People's dead relatives sometimes visit me – my messages aren't incredibly accurate, but it does feel like I'm meant to do something with this. Am I? I feel like it's a real privilege to be given these messages and abilities, so I want to make sure I honour them. But, how do I even share these messages with people? Sometimes they're so random, or for people I may not have been in touch with for ages, or only on Facebook. It seems weird to just send them a random message. Or am I meant to turn this off? How would I even do that? My grandmother used to get messages like this and, honestly, I think it really affected her. I know this kind of thing can be handed down across generations, so I don't want to mess it up – or have it mess me up, either.*

A You're right, this can be handed down across generations – but the truth is, it's handed down through *every* generation and *every* family, not just a select few. So, while it's marvellous this is something you feel bonded to your grandmother with, it is actually available to every single human being, in every single family. Whether or not everyone else is

171

aware of their abilities or ever chooses to do something with them is up to them, just as it's up to you. *You* get to decide how you want to use *your* gifts and abilities (psychic or otherwise).

Opting to develop your natural abilities must include developing boundaries, not just between you and the world of spirit, but also between you and others. Psychically reading someone without their consent isn't just uncool, it's downright violating, and will rack up some funky karma for you, too. Reading for others must always be with their consent, and with pure intentions.

That said, messages and impressions can come in even when we aren't seeking them. Receiving guidance we haven't specifically asked for, or that has been given to us from spirit without the consent of the subject, requires us to be very clear on our intent with that information once received. Knowledge is power; what you do with that power exposes your intentions. Discern how you will use such information. Strengthen your own energetic field and energy centres to reinforce your own energetic boundaries and surprise or uninvited messages won't drop in as often.

When spirit sees a doorway, it will come in – your job is to not leave it ajar. Not all spirits are benevolent (particularly the spirits of our deceased loved ones; generally higher guides and beings are far more benevolent). Some spirits will see an opportunity and pounce, luring you into their plans to convey messages, or trying to get you to buy into their energetic games. Limit this by grounding and protecting your own energy field, and be very clear about what energy from physical or non-physical beings you are willing to invite into your space.

And, in case I've completely freaked you out (I get it!), this hasn't been my experience. I don't allow in negative or lower vibrations – I have a specific 'bouncer guide' for that, and have worked to reinforce my energy. But, in the beginning, this was a big concern and something I actively worked on. I wasn't taking any chances!

Regain your power in these new communications. You are the keeper of your energy field, integrity and discernment in choosing how to interact with such messages. Here lies the potential lesson – this may not be about whether or not you must pass on messages, but instead it's teaching you whether or not you want to partake.

Passing on messages needs the receiver's permission, just as much as the medium must also give their permission. Remember, you aren't beholden to the world of spirit. You're not their message mule. You get to consent to this from a place of personal power and sovereignty. Just as every other person who receives or declines your messages does, too.

Sceptics unite!

Q *Aren't the two concepts of reincarnation and communicating with the spirits of the deceased in opposition to one another? How can our deceased loved ones be available to talk to in the spirit realm if they've reincarnated? Wouldn't that mean that they are now busy in another lifetime and not just hanging out in the ether waiting to chat with you? That's how I imagine it anyway. I struggle with this idea and I feel kinda sceptical, like you guys can't have it both ways.*

+ + . + . .

A Sceptics unite! Would you believe I'm actually naturally sceptical? Questioning everything, I think, is healthy. Or maybe it's just a hangover from my journalist training. Either way, this is the *exact* question I asked Chris very early on in the piece. I was looking for a way to discount what was happening to me in my awakening to spirit. Turns out, it's not the gotcha moment you may think it is.

To explain this concept, we have to stretch our understanding of time and space. On earth, in a physical body, we are limited to being in one place at one time. In the non-physical realm, for spirit and soul, they aren't bound by physicality and can technically be in multiple places at once. Without a body, it's all just energy, a frequency, that can move and bend throughout time and space. After physical death, our loved ones can move more freely through the ether, across time and space in a way that we can't really relate to so easily.

Another concept to help explain this possibility is the distinction between the soul and the spirit. The soul is the part of us that has lived many, many lifetimes and will likely go on to live many more. Soul is the part of us that reincarnates. Spirit, however, is very much linked to this lifetime, to this human form we are in. Connecting with a loved one then is more about tuning into the spirit of them than the soul. Both spirit and soul live on after physical death, but it's the distinction that makes both spirit communication and reincarnation possible.

We could also think of it this way. Even while we're still living in physical form, it's possible to communicate with our living loved ones not just physically, but also at a soul and spirit level. I can send messages to the spirit and soul of friends and family without using a phone or Facebook. It's possible to energetically communicate beyond our physical realm. We don't have to die to communicate in this way. I look forward to the day the rest of the world catches up with this – imagine the time saved scrolling!

I wasn't lying when I said I'd asked Chris this exact question – and added a twist. As I shared in *You Already*

Know, I communicated with my deceased family members, namely my Aunt Cathy, my granny and my grandad, despite never having physically met him as he died eleven years before I was born. I noticed that, over time, Cathy and Granny in particular didn't turn up as much anymore. Their energy wasn't as strong, or 'close', and I wondered if that meant they had now reincarnated. I suspect this to be true – however, all Chris would show me was that same picture I described at the start of this chapter: someone with arms folded, smirking. I also suspect that there is a point in our spiritual journey beyond the physical where peace is achieved and there's no involvement or attachment to our physical realm in quite the same way. I think it's why we're not all streaming information from old-world figures all the time (although, I think that would be pretty cool – a very different ancient history class!).

Life rolls on, we continue on one level and can find peace on another. Immense comfort can be found in that.

Spiritbook

Q *I've heard you say everyone has at least one spirit guide – but do they all work in cahoots? I follow different psychics and channels online who don't appear to know one another, and yet they often all talk about similar topics and themes at similar times. Maybe they're the ones in cahoots – I'm looking at you, Helen! Are all of our spirit guides relaying messages, especially to the professional psychics among us? Like is there some weird, wacky and wonderful spirit guide convention or meeting, where they all confer and confirm what information is shared at a particular time? How do these guides know what messages to give so all the psychics are relaying information at the same time?*

A Lol, I'd love to attend such a convention! Could you imagine? And, actually, Chris is saying you're not too far off the mark! Here's how he shows me it works.

First, individual spirit guides work with us personally to help each of us awaken and remember our life's path and purpose. They reconnect us to our inner world and guide us through internal change and transformation. This is essentially what I described and outlined in *You Already Know.*

Spirit guides, like people, don't work in isolation. There's a spiritual equivalent akin to Kevin Bacon's Six Degrees of Separation. Actually, as I write this, Chris clairvoyantly shows me an old Facebook promotional image depicting several interconnecting lines between generic profile pictures located all over the globe. While there's no 'Spiritbook' equivalent, they are all connected nonetheless, by six degrees or otherwise.

Guides all have 'jobs' or 'roles', but probably with better work conditions and no gender pay gap (although that implies there is gender in the world of spirit, which there is not – just a balance of masculine and feminine energies). Spirit guides have a mission, or purpose, too. Some are personal guides, while some are assigned other roles (like blueprint guides, or teacher guides, for example).

> **Blueprint guides** are members of your SST specifically charged with helping you remember, access and decode your own life manual, or soul blueprint. These beings were present when your soul made the very agreements detailed within the blueprint.

Other guiding beings are more interested in working at a collective level, a far bigger picture level beyond an individual's soul path. This is the category the High Council of Sages falls into. They are a group of guiding beings who act like an advisory board. The Council shares a common goal to work with a group of awakening beings on earth who are moving through huge change and spiritual growth. They are largely who I channel when I run my live channelling events or even sometimes on my podcast, *The Guided Collective*. As the word 'council' suggests, there is indeed a meeting of many guides, banding together to relay messages – but not quite a convention.

Such spiritual advisory boards are just like advisory boards here on the earthly plane, say like a business's board of directors. These spiritual councils are made up of individual guides with individual jobs, interests and possibly even agendas – but far less self-serving than we might perceive here. This is one of the reasons I call my group of personal spirit guides my Spiritual Support Team (SST) – it comprises a range of spirit guides, assigned to different roles. While it's possible such team members may potentially sit on other people's teams or boards, or councils, Chris tells me mine aren't working with any other psychics. Promise!

Where this starts to get even more complex is that the type of beings in the High Council of Sages are 'higher' than those beings in my personal SST. Or, more accurately, their role is higher (but it's not quite the hierarchy we understand here). Guides with a collective role aren't just interested in our personal evolution, but the evolution of humanity. So I wouldn't expect the High Council of Sages to give me personal advice, but they will help me understand just what is happening on our planet and to our collective consciousness, and what steps individuals need to take to better the collective. In that way, the beings of the High Council of Sages aren't 'mine' and, in fact, many of my community members have told me they've connected with them directly and received other messages. Wonderful! Is it possible other psychics or channels also connect with them? Absolutely! However, it's far more likely other psychics and channels are connecting with other councils or spiritual advisory boards. There's not just one!

Now, let's go up a few more levels. In my last book, I introduced the idea of the Soul Council. This is a similar concept. We can have an individual Soul Council – that is, a council of soul beings working for the advancement of our individual souls – and there is also a collective Soul Council, working for the collective soul's advancement. There is also an Earth Council, working to advance our earth, to aid and support and guide our earth's advancement and that's at the individual and collective level, too. And all these councils are working towards a collective earth blueprint – just like our individual soul blueprints, there is a blueprint outlining the growth, expansion and energetic up-levelling of our earth and all of humanity.

So, back to your original question – our guiding beings individually and collectively, depending on their level in the 'hierarchy', are all working towards the overarching blueprint and soul timeline of our earth. Thus, the messages received at an individual level are designed to bring each individual into their highest timeline, so the collective timeline improves, and is in line with the earth's blueprint. For we all chose to be here, on our earth, at this time, to experience and contribute to her growth and expansion.

Said more simply: yes, they're in cahoots – just maybe not like you were picturing.

Twinning

Q *Is there any special significance of a soul choosing to come in as a twin, or even a triplet? What about families with multiple multiple-births? Do twins have a different kind of experience of soul connections? For example, would they share a soul, a soul blueprint or even the same lessons and purpose? Do they come in together as twins to help one another with their souls' experiences? It's such an amazing part of our world, so I'm curious if it has an even greater significance in the bigger scheme of things, for souls.*

A When souls choose to come in together, say as twins, triplets or more, there is indeed a unique bond and experience, perhaps a deeper richness to the quality of the relationship and the bond between the souls incarnating. However, each individual has their own soul and therefore their own unique soul blueprint, with unique lessons, purpose and gifts.

For example, twins might choose to incarnate together to experience similar lessons, or purpose, but it's not a requirement. Twins could in fact choose to experience opposite sides of the same coin, for example, thus creating interesting dynamics within an incredibly close bond. Or the opposite could be true, and they are experiencing lessons around identity and self, within the confines of having an identical twin. Just imagine what lessons might be explored by twins who've been taught to do everything the same, right down to dating other identical twins!

Additionally, two (or more) souls may choose to incarnate together via a multiple birth to complete karma incurred in a previous lifetime. Perhaps the classroom established by choosing such a unique birthing and life bond creates the environment those souls need, or perhaps it has more to do with what that dynamic may mirror back to the rest of the family or other siblings in a way a typical family dynamic cannot. This could be chosen by the souls to allow them to complete – or initiate – a deeper exploration far beyond this lifetime.

Not every twin, or every multiple birth, has decided to experience their soul lessons and purpose together. These souls could just as easily choose to come in for the parents, or family, they are being born into. The lessons and purpose may not necessarily be for the twins themselves, but for the parents to learn lessons of unconditional love, for example, or to explore how to raise children without assuming who they are, a lesson that a hypothetical parent may find challenging if they were to have identical twins staring back at them.

An interesting side note here in terms of astrology: souls choose the timing of their arrival. This is captured by astrological placements at the time of birth. So, depending on how close together the children are born, their astrology would be incredibly similar, if not almost identical. However, it's safe to say that not every person with similar astrology would experience the world in the same way. So it is with twins and their blueprints. There will be similarities, but each individual – and their individual souls – will express themselves in the world quite differently. And one soul can't complete the mission on behalf of the other one, no matter what kind of fun identical-twin-swapping shenanigans they've used to fool humans.

QUESTIONS TO ASK YOURSELF

You might like to meditate on the following questions, use them as journalling prompts, invite your own SST to answer you, or turn an oracle card from The Little Sage Oracle Cards in response.

* How does my SST like to get my attention?
* Are there loved ones in the spirit world surrounding me?
* How will I know my SST or loved ones are present?
* How can I connect more with spirit? (Journalling? Oracle cards? Meditation?)
* What does my soul feel like?
* What does my spirit feel like?
* What information do I most need to know from my higher guidance right now?

If these questions and answers prompt a deeper enquiry, I've compiled a list of additional resources at helenjacobs. co/ask.

Keep the faith

Life can be just plain hard. No doubt, we've all felt like giving up, or giving in, at one point or another. You won't be the first, or the last, to wonder what it's all for. When we feel hopeless and helpless, like the world is going up in flames (figuratively and literally), how do we keep the faith that it's still all part of some bigger plan?

Such a line of questioning has become more and more frequent. And that's probably not surprising. As I write this in late 2020, our faith has been tested in a way it may never have been. The year's events brought into stark contrast the intersection of individual rights and collective needs. Chris shows me there comes a point in our awakening when we realise we are not separate; what happens 'over there' is really happening 'over here', too. And so the questions have to eventually become bigger than us if we're doing this awakening thing right.

Straight up: keeping the faith can be just as freaking hard as the hard stuff we're experiencing. There's no one-size-fits-all faith manual. How I keep the faith may look and feel entirely differently from your practice. And, honestly, that's kind of the point. Souls come to this planet for a certain kind of experience. Incarnating here is all about duality and the perceived separateness from ourselves, each other and our source. It is through that kind of separation from the whole, from the source (which often comes with doubt and disassociation), that we find our way back. Our time here on earth actually allows our souls the opportunity to explore faith as a core tenet of the time here. This is true at an individual level, but now we are seeing it more acutely at a collective level, too. Faith is an incredibly personal experience and so, in sharing the questions and answers in this chapter, my hope is you may find a new line of enquiry to weave into your own life.

Most of all, I want to remind you of this: it's okay to want to give up, or give in. It's what we do with that feeling that's important. You're not alone. Reach out, get support. Even if all the faith you can muster right now is that there is someone else who has a little extra to spare. Let someone else's faith be enough for you in those moments you can't muster enough faith for yourself.

Learning fatigue

Q *My girlfriend and I have been on and off for a few years now. We repeat the same pattern – we get together, say we'll do things differently and a few months later our same shit comes back to haunt us. We're currently off again, which is okay with me. My question is not so much about her (I'm protecting myself and my heart from her right now) but more about the lessons. You say lessons keep repeating and so I guess I'm just not learning this lesson – but that's not exactly motivating me right now. I wasn't the best learner at school, so now I'm trying to look to a bigger guidance and I can't help but feel I'm failing here, too. How can we keep trusting and believing things are going to change when the same thing just keeps on happening? If I really don't go back this time, will I have learned my lesson?*

A I struggle with this idea of lessons, too – not so much the concept, but the word. In truth, I don't have a better word to use. Spirit speaks to me in impressions; I try to relay those messages through our language, and the word 'lesson' is the closest word I've got. It's hugely inadequate, though, because it implies that we will be graded, just like in school. But, to spirit, there is no failing, not even a sliding grade-scale. Judgement, as we know it, doesn't exist for spirit, so we cannot fail. Judgement is a far more human construct: right or wrong; pass or fail; win or lose. From the perspective of our guides and soul, it's all learning. So right now, your soul is happy. You're questioning, learning, exploring – and that sounds a lot more like winning than failing to soul.

Of course, it's still just plain hard to your human self when you're in the throes of it all. It's always okay to feel what you're feeling – but don't let it define you and don't stay in that feeling for too long. Feeling like a failure, feeling defeated or struggling to figure it all out begs for a starting point of forgiveness, love and acceptance of yourself.

You're not missing something everyone else has figured out. In fact, *this belief* may indeed be the lesson, more than the relationship itself. It's just a mirror. Behaviours stem from beliefs. Believing you're a failure becomes a self-fulfilling prophecy (not a psychic one!). Change the belief, change the behaviour, change the outcome.

One last point: after doing the belief work, check if you still need to protect your heart. With clearer boundaries, physically and energetically, you'll be better placed to handle the flux with your on-and-off-again girlfriend. You may not want her back into your space, but you won't need to shut her – or anyone else – out. The opposite is actually true. Doing the inner work (like such belief work) reinforces our true nature, which at its core is unconditional love – and we never need to protect ourselves from that.

Manifesting mojo

Q *Can you please explain to me this idea of manifesting because I must be doing something wrong. I've got the vision board. I charge my crystals. I use mantras and positive affirmations and I'm always trying to be positive and give out good energy. But, nothing has manifest into my life the way I want. I'm still stuck in the same job. The cash isn't rolling in. And I've been single for too long. Everyone says manifesting is putting out what you want to get back, but I feel like I'm giving way more than I'm getting. What am I missing?*

A Manifesting gets a bad rap, mainly I believe because it's generally so poorly articulated. Spirit shows me that our current understanding of manifesting here in our earthly realm is still in its infancy and we're yet to fully grasp how to work with this concept in much more powerful ways. So, no, you're not missing anything; you're wading through incredibly confusing information.

Manifesting is much more than thinking good thoughts and doing good things. Manifesting has far more to do with our energy (or frequency, or vibration) and the belief *behind* those good thoughts and good things. Thinking good thoughts alone won't attract much, because your energy field can still be riddled with holes or negativity or stagnation, or your actions can be misaligned with those good thoughts. For example, doing kind things for others purely out of obligation or a hope that the favour will be returned won't amount to much. A sieve can't catch you much water.

For manifesting to work, you must have alignment between your thoughts, actions and energy. And, I would add, what you want to manifest must be aligned with your soul and its blueprint. No matter how much we desire something, if it's not aiding our soul's growth and advancement in accordance with the areas we came in to explore, if it's not aligned with our soul's blueprint, no amount of positivity or 'good vibes' can make it happen. Soul trumps all.

Desiring a relationship is one thing; desiring your soulmate to journey deeper into your soul agreements is another. You must be committed to that powerful alignment, not simply visualising Mr Tall-Dark-and-Handsome. Vision boards and affirmations are not enough without the energetic magnetism and soul alignment to give them the equivalent geomagnetic pull you need.

When I'm manifesting, I work on these three things.

1. What do you really desire?

Become intimately familiar with what this desire *feels* like, where you feel it in your body and what it feels like to increase that feeling. Clarity turns the manifesting magnet on and amplifies its pulling power. Shooting for a feeling leaves the *how* and the *what* open. For example, if I want to manifest a new home, I'm not visualising the specifics of a white picket fence and luxury bathrooms. I'm tuning into how it feels in that home – comforting, safe, abundant, peaceful, for example. I focus on the feeling, and life will start working on bringing me solutions that match that feeling. And as solutions begin to appear, I amend my feeling to bring the exact match.

2. Don't turn off your desire

All other thoughts, actions and energy in opposition to this feeling detract from your magnetism, or weaken its magnetic pull. That's why it's important we clear, heal and restore these parts of ourselves that are in opposition to what we desire. I explored this concept in detail in *You Already Know* when I introduced the Guidance Cycle.

The **Guidance Cycle** refers to a predictable pattern of clearing, healing, restoring and manifesting that our guidance from our intuition and our SST will lead us through. We must be able to clear and heal, then restore our energy, in order to manifest what is next along our life path. I've included additional information on page 262 to help you explore where you might be in the cycle and the next steps to take.

Following your guidance will eventually lead you through this cycle of clearing, healing and restoring so that you're best able to manifest. And this clearing, healing and restoring must be addressed across all areas of your physical, mental, emotional and spiritual bodies. Suffice to say, constant energetic improvement rapidly improves your manifesting ability. So, when I'm desiring a home with comfort and abundance, but I have limiting beliefs, life will present opportunities to deal with them, so I can come back to my manifesting.

3. Trust it's coming

Imagine actually receiving your desires. Imagine your life suddenly flooded with all the richness of relationships and the satisfaction of your work and the joy of an ever-abundant bank account. How would that feel? Not just what you *think* it would feel like, but how does your body actually respond? As you imagine receiving this, your mind doesn't know if it's real or not. And so your body will give you a clue as to its response – how does it feel? Could you cope with the influx of receiving the higher vibration of everything you desire? As crazy as it sounds, we're not really wired for such high vibes, or at least sustaining them for any great lengths of time. *Yet.* That's what this mass awakening is for – it just took a global pandemic to get enough of us to pay attention.

Your body must be primed and ready to receive that amount of joy, abundance and love, and sustain it for longer and longer periods of time. And the way to increase your capacity for this is to move through your internal transformation by clearing, healing and restoring – try the Guidance Cycle I just mentioned.

Ultimately it is this *frequency of desire*, not the positive thoughts or actions, that is what you're really putting out and what you will therefore get back. As you move through this process, you'll refine your desires, ensuring the ego's wants give way to your soul's true desires. Depending on which frequency you cultivate, the results will be so very different.

Chasm of chaos

Q *I get that we are meant to trust that everything is happening for us, but I find this such a hard concept in practice. There's so much hurt and pain in the world right now, I just can't seem to reach a point where I can accept this is a good thing. How exactly are we meant to keep the faith, or continue trusting spirit or our guidance when the evidence before us is absolute chaos and disarray? I truly want to have faith in what my spirit guides, or my intuition, are telling me but I'm just finding that incredibly hard given everything that's going on in the world at the moment. How do I cultivate trust in myself and in the process of life? It's hard.*

A Agreed. This lovely sentiment is a little tough, especially right now. Even though our minds can intellectually understand the concept that everything is happening *for* our highest good, our bodies aren't always so quick to agree. Knowing something is different from believing it, let alone wholeheartedly living it. For us to fully embody a concept such as this, we need to move through an internal integration process to increase our level of consciousness, so we see ourselves as part of the whole that exists to support us, our growth and our existence.

We are actually moving through this integration en masse right now. Mass integration is just as messy as an individual integration, and suddenly amplified. We are in the collective messy middle of change, and we can't see the other side of it yet. It's hard to believe this is working for us, when we can't see how. *Yet.*

My motto is always to start small. So, if you're looking at building trust in what is happening in our world right now, it's the equivalent of trying to drive a car before you can even crawl. Start with something smaller in your own immediate life. Can you tweak the smallest aspect of your days to help you see how things work out for you – a traffic delay is actually a blessing when you realise you missed a crash, or losing your job turns out to be the butt-kick towards your side hustle.

Our minds crave proof. Look for the silver linings and you won't just see them, but *expect* them. When you expect them for yourself, and you're used to having them fulfilled, it's not such a stretch to start believing and expecting such solutions for our world, too.

Faith and trust, by their very nature, ask us to believe in something we cannot see, we cannot touch – something that isn't physically real in three dimensions yet. We can find it when we trust that a flower will grow or, equally, that the weeds will find a way through those cracks. So can you, and all of life.

All of life is born out of the unknown, out of the void, the nothingness, the chasm. Faith bridges the chasm between knowledge and lived experience.

Stay woke

Q *I don't know if I want to keep drinking this spiritual Kool-Aid. I want to give up. Not on life, but on this way of thinking. I've been on this 'spiritual journey' for a few years now. But awakening is much harder than I expected and I don't want to keep seeing the world through this lens. It was easier when I wasn't 'awake' – because now I have to really face things. I thought it was all meant to become much easier, but frankly it's all too fucking hard. Can I just go back to sleep?*

A Asleep, awake, or somewhere in between: the choice is yours.

You're right. Following our guidance and doing the inner work means things get messy, fast. You're not the first, nor the last, who'll want to turn back. Are you also someone who starts to drive to your friend's house, only to turn around halfway because you no longer like the route, or it's taking too long, or you're not sure you really like your friend anymore anyway? Maybe you are.

Frustration and resistance along this pathway are actually good signs – and they put you closer to a breakthrough than you realise. As much as you may want to avoid your problems, or progress, it's not so great in the long run. Whatever we avoid catches up with us eventually and, when it does, it usually makes its presence known far bigger and stronger than before. I'd rather be woken by a gentle tickle than a sledgehammer.

Going back to sleep is also a disservice to those around you. Your inner transformation and spiritual awakening aren't just for you; they are about playing your role in the greater awakening. Share your gifts. Make your impact. Go wake up those still sleeping (preferably with a gentle tickle than with a sledgehammer).

Awakening is the whole damn point. We all have to do it at some point; and if not this life, then the next. But, it's not just the transition from slumber to waking – what will you do once you're awake?

One last point on giving up – you don't have to do this alone. Call in the physical and spiritual support teams you need. Your physical support team may look like health professionals, therapists and energy workers (or even family, friends and in-home help) and, of course, your spiritual support team is made up of the higher beings you call on to work with you.

QUESTIONS TO ASK YOURSELF

You might like to meditate on the following questions, use them as journalling prompts, invite your own SST to answer you, or turn an oracle card from The Little Sage Oracle Cards in response.

* What do I know for sure?
* What are my fundamental core beliefs? (And do they truly serve me?)
* Who, or what, do I turn to when things are hard?
* Who turns to me when things are hard for them? How do I best show up for them? And what might I need to do for myself to manage that?

If these questions and answers prompt a deeper enquiry, I've compiled a list of additional resources at helenjacobs. co/ask.

Good versus bad

I've avoided writing this chapter. There, I said it. I, too, have resistance! Here, I've compiled those curly questions that, even though I've been asked them so many times before, I always find the hardest to answer. They are often the hardest for us to accept and digest, too. And I'd hate to be the messenger who does get shot.

So, here you'll find those hard questions, such as why do bad things happen to good people, why is there inequality and injustice, and why would soul choose all this? Recognising my own privilege while I answer these questions feels even more squeamish. Working with these feelings and processing our own resistance – and privilege – is exactly how we move through such blindingly glaring disparities in our world. The times are finally demanding it of each of us.

Receiving spirit's answers to these questions can be eye-opening and just plain challenging. We need to move beyond our individual discomforts and into the discomforts of our world if we want to make real, lasting change. This is the point, at both a micro and macro level, that helps us fulfil what all souls come here to do: realise we are all one and the same, we are all connected and that to love one another is truly to love ourselves, and vice versa. Separatism cannot survive, nor can the individual over the group. Our world is showing us this via many mirrors right now – we cannot look away.

What I share here are snippets. In no way are these comprehensive, all-encompassing, definitive answers to the big questions. Instead, may they serve as thought provokers, conversation starters and, more importantly, action prompters for you. And, I'll warn you, some of the content may be triggering for some readers (please take care if you think this will be the case for you).

So, buckle up, this is big.

The goodness formula

Q *I have a two-parter for you. I was raised to believe that if I did all the right things then life would somehow reward me. Because good things happen to good people. I believe I'm a good person, so why do bad things happen to me? I'm not talking about terrible things, just the mundane. Nothing ever turns out for me.*

On the other hand, what about people who aren't so good – and yet get away with it? What about murderers? Abusers? What happens to these once-innocent infants who then become monsters? If religion and spirituality profess forgiveness, how do we forgive the unforgivable?

A Somewhere along the line we learned a certain formula that said 'do good things = get good things = good person'. But this formula is broken. It's flawed at worst and simply limited at best. Good things are not just magically handed out to people who are 'good'. Who is good? Who is bad? Is goodness only measured by what you *do*? And who the hell is deciding? Santa has a lot of explaining to do ...

Spirit's perspective on 'goodness' is not based on what you *do* but on who you *are* at your core. You are good because you're here, because you're an extrapolation of the source. You are divinity in motion. A person's worth and value cannot be measured by their actions – or mistakes – alone. Thus, at our core, we are all 'good'.

Alas, we humans are not accustomed to seeing people at their core. Instead, we view things through ego and judgement; we peg people according to their actions (or what they have, the money in their bank account, or the label on their clothing – or if they have clothing at all). Because we see life this way, we have confused or assumed that the realm of spirit, or some God Almighty, must also see it this way. Raised by a Catholic mother and an atheist father and destined to become a psychic, I've had to find my place with my personal spiritual and religious beliefs. Twelve years of Catholic schooling and church attendance resulted in quite a religious upbringing to unravel as I arrived at my own conclusions. I unsubscribed from this idea of God Almighty judging us from on high (and, frankly, found it largely benefited the patriarchy, rather than all the people it purported to support).

We are not the sum of our actions. These actions are what allow us to learn and grow, both as a human and a soul. It seems counterproductive to send us forth to learn – and then punish us for doing what we came here to do. What we choose to do with our mistakes is more important than the mistake itself. Expecting to live without making mistakes, without making choices that may hurt or disappoint others, or ourselves, will prohibit a truly happy life. We will never measure up, because that definition of good is aligned with a perfection we were never designed to experience or live by (but one that perhaps kept someone else feeling more powerful over others by requiring they measure up).

To anticipate the second part of this question – all people are created equal, but not all of our mistakes and actions are equal. Of course, the truly heinous actions of murder and abuse should be held accountable in our world. But does that make those individuals 'bad' as a result? They, too, have the option and opportunity for repentance, recovery and reconciliation. Just as we all do, they have choices – and the choices made after such heinous actions may be a truer measure of the individual.

Such judgement is absent in the realm of spirit. There is no hierarchy requiring the lower levels perform to the liking of someone deemed more powerful, higher or better. Instead, the accountability lies within the individual. And there's a world of difference between accountability and judgement. Spirit doesn't have a punishment system; I'm yet to see the god-like figure, proclaiming eternal punishments in some fiery hell. Even the concepts of heaven and hell are flawed – spirit shows that heaven is akin to our alignment to our divinity, and hell a kind of suffering from being so far removed from it. It exists inside of us, not 'out there' for some all-knowing being to determine our fate.

Let me be clear: there's no green light to intentionally do harm, to do 'bad' things to others. Blatantly, consciously, knowingly *choosing* to harm another causes obvious harm to the other person, but also an incredible amount of karma to the perpetrator. Karma is not just 'what goes around comes around'; it is a deep etching in the soul's blueprint holding the soul to account. Those lessons will be learned, the inner healing will eventually occur, and energetically the scales will be balanced.

A lack of 'bad' things would stunt growth. We would not experience the duality we came to earth to experience. To the soul, the 'bad' things the human perceives are the very things soul sees as a gift. Without that hardship, there is no lesson to learn at all.

Abundant poverty

Q *Why is there so much poverty in our world? It saddens me to see so many people live in squalor, without basic sanitation, without food, water and shelter. Families losing children to disease that is preventable – families becoming families because the birthrate is not preventable. If this is such an abundant world, why is such a vast proportion of the world's population living below the poverty line, in such horrendous conditions? Why would souls choose that as the life to incarnate into? Will this ever change?*

A Let's not confuse an abundant world with the greed of humans. Our planet has provided for all; humans have portioned and profited from the unequal distribution of that natural abundance. Every soul has a right to share in the abundance of the planet we've incarnated on. Our universe is ever-expanding with an ever-replenishing abundance. What interrupts this flow of growth and expansion is us – humans. How our earth's abundance of natural resources and money is managed and circulated has become an issue of human greed, power and misuse. No one person or group has been deemed better custodians of these resources. But humans have confused this over time. Poverty exists because humans allow it.

Souls incarnating on this planet at this time are aware of the existing parameters of the world they are visiting. Poverty creates an unusual environment for a soul to incarnate into and the establishment of conditions to explore deeper lessons. For example, humans may struggle with the idea of poverty because of the common modern misconception that money equates to happiness. Spirit, however, debates that money alone leads to a better quality of life. If a soul incarnates into a life of less financially, it doesn't mean a life of less meaning, depth, joy and fulfilment. Instead, it may allow karma to be balanced, and for explorations around true abundance – or around lack.

We humans may perceive poverty to mean these people are experiencing less – but it's hard to tell through a human viewpoint alone if these souls are actually more mature, exploring what it means to have non-attachment, to have a deeper connection to their bodies, to value safety and trust, and to understand the importance of joy and perception. We could be looking at it all wrong. Perhaps souls who've experienced great material wealth in previous lifetimes now opt to enjoy a life of less material accumulation. We don't reach enlightenment through things.

Conversely, we must ask why would a soul choose to experience material abundance and financial wealth? Surely not just for the pleasure of hoarding what money we have?!

What onus is on the soul with more? What choices, actions and behaviours will these individuals take to balance the scales? To redistribute wealth, to ensure sanitation and access to education and opportunity, to fight for change, not just observe poverty 'over there'? Poverty continues to exist because it's not a problem for those who don't experience it. And souls who are willingly ignoring it are also accumulating karma. This great awakening now is demanding the privileged do more to restore balance.

No matter whether a soul has incarnated to explore either lack or abundance, all must awaken and remember the role we must play in changing the disparity and inequality we see.

Our world improves not only when there is more equality and equitable access to shared resources (and equality across races, genders, sexuality and so on), but when those who benefit from the very systems and structures upholding the inequality fight to have them removed.

Forgiving the unforgivable

Q *Teachings on forgiveness suggest that, as a victim of abuse, I am simply meant to forgive the person who did this to me. But I can't. I didn't ask for it. I didn't deserve it. This was something a monster did to me ... and I'm expected to just forgive and move on? How? I have to live with this for the rest of my life while I cannot see an impact for him at all. He has not received punishment; his life has not been derailed. This is not fair and I absolutely have a right to be angry about it. I'm sick of people telling me my anger isn't helpful. Why should I be the one to suffer – and still have to do the forgiving?*

A You're absolutely right. You did not ask to be abused. You did not deserve – *no one* deserves – to be abused. You were absolutely on the other end of another human's actions and their actions have had devastating impacts on your life. Spirit cannot be more plain on this point: you are not limited or bound by another's decisions, choices and actions and they implore you to see your life as far more than this.

What if forgiveness was not about letting your abuser off the hook, but instead it was a road to freedom for you? What if forgiveness didn't condone or accept your abuser's behaviour, but it had far more to do with *you*? Forgiveness means giving yourself permission to lean into something *more* for you, some other possibility beyond the pain and hurt you're accustomed to. Your freedoms were once compromised, but they needn't continue to be. Only you can decide if this will ever get better for you. And only you can make it so. Your future is not set in stone. What you do next is your choice.

Somewhere along the line, I heard the adage that gripping onto a blade and hoping someone else bleeds is the same as not wanting to forgive. Hanging on to your anger, however justified and understandable it is, will only go on hurting you. Your anger doesn't punish your abuser, it's continuing to punish you, for something you hold no culpability in whatsoever.

Pain can be a portal, a gateway, deeper into our selves and our soul. And yet, we don't think of our pain like that, do we? We just want to avoid it, mask it, run from it or hope we can project and transfer it onto others. No one wants to stay locked in the pain. The only way is through. Please look into the specific techniques and supports – physically, mentally, emotionally and energetically (and at a soul level, too) – to transform the pain and trauma. A therapist will be well trained to support you. You don't need to do this alone.

Anger, just like pain, is another portal. Emotional embodiment (actually deeply feeling your emotions) can act as a gateway to your healing, freedom and liberation.

Pain, anger and all your other emotions suggest where there is room to let go, heal, forgive. Your emotions can also high-light what you really want. Your anger may be suggesting what you no longer want – and there is indeed so much more here for you.

Your choice has not been permanently removed. Right now you get to choose how you want the rest of your life to go. You get to decide the kinds of people, love and relation-ships you wish to call into your life from here on in. You get to choose to protect yourself – and possibly even others – by the choices you make today. Your power may have been taken away in the moments of abuse; how are you going to reclaim your power and remember how strong you are now, and forever more?

Soul's choice

Q *I've heard you say our soul chose this life. We chose our parents, lessons and so on. Mine appear to be manageable – but why on earth would a soul choose to incarnate and experience poverty, abuse, neglect or harm? I just can't make peace with that. Why do some souls choose something so much harder?*

+ . + . .

A At the surface level, it may indeed appear that some souls choose to incarnate with harder lessons and tougher experiences than others. However, what we see at the human level is not always as it seems to the soul. Here are a few reasons why souls would choose what appear to be harder lessons.

Soul evolution

Souls are at varying degrees of soul maturity, based on the number of lives lived. Some are very new souls (new to earth), some are older souls. A newer soul may choose to experience what is perceived to be an easier life. Imagine if this was a soul's first time here – they're like a tourist, taking it all in, enjoying the scenery, taking soul selfies. Newer souls may not have racked up karma, because they haven't had any, or very few, previous lifetimes on earth. This means they're 'untouched' by the world, so they aren't arriving with any deeper soul 'baggage'.

That's not to say, though, that mature souls are the only ones with all the hardship. Mature souls may be balancing the scales across lifetimes, or may be exploring another side of a particular soul lesson that requires a 'harder' life. But, just as easily, this more mature soul could choose to experience an easier life – a 'breather', if you will, a chance to rest and recoup between 'harder' lifetimes.

Karma

There's a generalised perception that karma rewards or punishes. However, I see it differently. Karma doesn't mean that 'good' souls from one life are automatically rewarded with a 'better' life next time – a 'good' life last time may actually allow for a 'harder' life this time, so the soul can continue exploring in a different way. Growth is often through the challenges and the lessons. As I explored in the answer on page 205 there's no judgement and judicial system in the spirit world. Karma simply means at some point things will balance out.

Tutoring

Some souls are students; some teachers. Of course, we're all learning and teaching, but in different lifetimes we may have a particular predisposition to one of these roles. Certain soul agreements may require some souls to teach more, while others will have far more to learn. A dear client of mine comes to mind here; she and I often joke that in this lifetime her soul signed on for what most souls accomplish over many, many lifetimes. Being student or teacher can influence the level of 'hardship' we encounter this time around.

Soul gifts

What humans perceive as challenging people, relationships and situations, soul sees as gifts. When someone wrongs us, or hurts us, our human response is disbelief, hurt and anger. Our soul, however, can see this person not as the enemy, but as a soul ally – for they have loved us so much to ensure we've learned the lesson we agreed to explore together. Thus, the choice of a 'harder' life, or a lot of lessons, is a much deeper consideration than what may be deemed easy or hard.

Why bother?

Q *You say soul comes here for its development, that we have free will to choose and ultimately everything is for soul's advancement. So, to soul there is no right or wrong, good or bad. Then soul completes its time here and returns to wherever it has come from – and then there is no judgement of our earthly experiences. So, what's the point? If all souls are equal to begin with, why come to earth and play this winner-less game, if it doesn't amount to much anyway? Am I missing something in this theory?*

A Let me share a clairvoyant metaphor Chris gave me years ago to help illustrate this point. He calls this metaphor, or analogy, the Mothership.

Picture a spaceship of sorts, the Mothership, which comes to earth. Inside the Mothership is the Great Mother. Hovering above the earth and looking around, the Great Mother realises there's a lot of ground to cover, so much to experience. The Great Mother wants to explore all facets of earth and realises that she cannot achieve all that on her own. She decides to clone herself so she can cover more ground in less time.

218

Instead of cloning mirror images of herself, the Great Mother programs billions of individuals. Each has the same essence as the Great Mother, but she makes tweaks so each is likely to have a varied experience, thus helping her to explore more than she ever would alone. Same same but different. The Great Mother then assigns each clone a specific mission and programs each with the skills necessary to undertake their mission. The Great Mother instructs each clone to report in to the Mothership and not to each other. And away they go, down to earth.

The Great Mother remains in the Mothership, witnessing the scene on earth. As the clones make their way from the cosmos to earth, their assignments are wiped from their memory. Each clone vaguely recollects their specific assignment, but it's too unclear to commit to wholeheartedly. Forgetting they can go within and read through the internal dialogue pre-programmed by the Great Mother, these clones begin looking around at each other for clues to their assignment. Watching on, the Great Mother realises it's not playing out according to the plan – and yet it's fascinating nonetheless. This experience of earth is far greater than she ever could have imagined on her own.

Sooner or later, the Great Mother calls the clones back one by one to the Mothership and they review the clone's time on earth. At this point, the clone's memory is again intact and it can see whether it was successful in its mission. The Great

Mother can always resend the clone to try again, to complete another mission, or perhaps tweak the suit she sends the clone off in or alter the mission slightly.

And so it is with life. Just like the clone, our soul's job is to follow out the assignment of the universe, the assignment from source. We are sent forth to experience various aspects – you focus on love, they focus on forgiveness, this one's a cheerleader – and all the data is fed back to the source, thus accomplishing far more than we can on our own. We are all part of the whole, learning how we fit together, as one and as separate entities.

The *experience* is far more important than the judgement of the experience – and the experiences to be had on earth are not available in the realm of spirit, because it exists in different dimensions, with different limitations, the absence of physicality being one of them.

QUESTIONS TO ASK YOURSELF

You might like to meditate on the following questions, use them as journalling prompts, invite your own SST to answer you, or turn an oracle card from The Little Sage Oracle Cards in response.

* Why have bad things happened in my life?
* Why have good things happened in my life?
* What privileges do I have in my life? What do I plan to do with them?
* What problems do I wish to help solve in the world?
* Who, or what, do I need to forgive? Am I ready to do that?

If these questions and answers prompt a deeper enquiry, I've compiled a list of additional resources at helenjacobs. co/ask.

Collective issues

There's no denying we are living through a remarkable period in our human existence and evolution. Notably, the types of questions and discussions among my clients and community have sharply changed. We've reached a tipping point of awakening. Hoorah!

However, such change is uncomfortable. We can't just magically snap our fingers to arrive at the end outcome (trust me, I've tried). Change requires we *actually change* – both individually and collectively. We are in the messy middle of collective, mass awakening.

In *You Already Know*, I compared a personal awakening with being in a darkened room with a blindfold on and the curtains drawn, then being spun around three times and asked to make our way out of the room without being injured.

We're all now in the same cramped room.

Individually, we must be responsible for our own inner world transformation. We must review our belief systems and question our behaviours and how they impact us and others. Perhaps the irony of experiencing a period of pandemic isolation was realising we cannot, and must not, live in isolation. We are all important threads of a greater ecosystem, or a beautiful tapestry. We all play a part.

Collectively, we must weave together what we've come to see during our own personal awakenings. As I write this book, protesters fight for racial equality, parts of our world are still in lockdown as a result of the COVID-19 pandemic and my homeland is still recovering from catastrophic climate fires. There are countless movements aiming to do just that – *move us*.

For years now, a collective awakening has been occurring. Somewhat quietly to begin with – but now the whole damn house is waking up, clanging in the kitchen and urging those still slumbering to get out of bed. If this is our collective rebirth, then we're truly deep in labour. It's painful as hell, but there's only one way out. *Push*.

Supporting supporters

Q *How do we best support others during these really difficult times, especially our kids? As we lived through the challenges of COVID-19 and the lockdowns and social distancing, I saw many people around me struggle, especially the children in my life. We may not even know the true impacts of this time for many years to come. How are we going to be able to take care of everyone else, those more vulnerable, like children, when many of us adults aren't doing so great ourselves?*

A No matter the times we live in, if we want to best support someone else, we must ensure we've first taken care of ourselves as best we can – physically, mentally, emotionally and spiritually. We cannot give what we do not have. And what we have to give may not be an exact match for what another needs. For example, we may not be able to support someone's mental health but perhaps we are financially able to contribute. Or perhaps our emotional stability creates a safe place for others to express and vent.

As the long-lasting implications of this pandemic reveal themselves to us, and I've made several predictions on this elsewhere (you can find them on *The Guided Collective* podcast, if you're interested), we must remember that difficult times create great change. Every single one of us has chosen to be on the earth at this time, to experience this, to contribute to this and indeed to learn from this. Once again, the challenge at the human level is the gift at the soul level.

Specifically for our kids, we must remember how strong and resilient they are. An entire generation is being shaped by this, both in 'positive' and potentially 'negative' ways – but, to soul it's all good. To soul, these are exactly the lessons and timings they signed on for. Imagine what they're here to do with this!

Supporting children right now may look like remembering we need the village, although ironically the village was stripped away during lockdowns. These little souls were brave enough to incarnate, to experience this and to fight for change. They've chosen to be here for our liberation! They have chosen to partake in such significant, tremendous change. This is not necessarily a sacrifice as there is no martyrdom to soul, but a deep commitment and willingness to do this.

We can support our kids by modelling our own growth, asking for help when we – or they – need it. And not losing faith. We need it now more than ever.

But I'm an empath

Q *Everything happening in our world right now is all a bit too much for me. I'm sensitive and an empath and I get too overwhelmed with all this energy and angst. I don't like to read the news because it just feels so sad and overwhelming. I feel the pain of everyone around me, I feel it all, and I'm not sure I can keep feeling all of this. How can we sensitive souls best contribute in these times without collapsing beneath the weight of it all?*

A The term 'empath' is often bandied about as a catch-all for anyone who feels an emotion, or feels sympathy or empathy for others. For want of a better word, it is also used to describe individuals who are highly attuned to the energetic vibration or state of others and our world. There is a distinction.

Right now, every empath feeling the vibrational shift *should* be overwhelmed. Tuning out and ignoring the state of our world, and the billions of people within it, is not a long-term strategy. It is not a stance that supports anyone in any meaningful way – what good are our empath tendencies if they do not awaken us to our brothers and sisters in need? Where does our spirituality go then?

To be sure, there are times when our own mental health, or physical, emotional or spiritual health, needs to be the priority. There are moments for pause and reprieve, but those moments cannot be the norm. And they should only be there to help buoy us into further action once more.

Feeling overwhelmed and *choosing* to opt out is a luxury and privilege that those actually *experiencing* the very challenges, hardship and anguish the news reports do not have. For them, this pain you're feeling is their everyday occurrence and not something they can switch off at whim. Their pain *should* be your pain; we are not separate.

Rather than collapsing from the overwhelm, we must choose to strengthen our internal energetic structures to face it. An overwhelmed energetic field is simply suggesting there is further work to do – not that the work must be somebody else's to do.

Constant attention to our internal and energetic structures allows us to be fully present, to stay present to the pain, the discomfort and the challenge, and to stay present to those around us. Use that same empath skill to tune into those higher, healing vibrations. Run them through your system; run that energy through the earth's energy grids.

Then, remember the unique gifts you incarnated with, which were bestowed upon you so you would be able to contribute to the change the planet is moving through – for every soul knew of this ahead of time. To our souls, this is not a surprise! The more energetically sensitive among us may have been sent here to work the energies. Some as activists, lobbyists, teachers, healers, mothers … we all play a role. Ignorance and denial, however, are not options.

We aren't healing ourselves for our own gain, as lovely as it may be. We are healing ourselves to continue offering our energy, our time and our resources towards the change we're here to make. And that means that when we have more of those things we are actually better placed to help others up – not get overwhelmed by their situation and feel inadequately placed to contribute.

Climate change

Q *As 2020 began, it seemed like the world really started to realise that climate change is happening* now. *Suddenly, the world was captivated by the Australian bushfires, and change felt possible. Then, of course, the global pandemic arrived and the world's attention shifted. Will climate change come back onto the agenda? Will we actually see change in our climate, in our world, to help sustain life on our planet? What is spirit's perspective on climate change?*

+ + . + . .

A While they appear unrelated, these issues are all moving us in the same direction. The overall goal is upgrading the energy on our planet, to move us from a three-dimensional reality into higher dimensions and higher consciousness. All the social, political and environmental movements are taking us there. Spirit sees them all working in unison towards the same goal, like a multi-faceted tapestry only complete once all the pieces are woven together.

Climate change needs our attention; we need to counter-balance and course-correct our actions and attitudes. Although media headlines have shifted, climate change is still being addressed, especially by those whose souls are assigned to weave these pieces of the tapestry together. As everyone remembers their soul's mission or purpose – the contribution they came here to make to the collective mission of raising consciousness – then real change can sweep through. It's so much bigger than climate change or a global health crisis alone. And it's far bigger than any one individual's purpose – we all have a role to play, and it starts with taking responsibility for our individual part, then weaving ourselves into the greater tapestry of life.

The pandemic shifted people's awareness of core issues in the world. It has quickly highlighted great disparities in our societies and cultures; illustrated what reprieve our environment receives when travel and gas emissions are limited; created waves within education and workplace structures that weren't functioning; and prompted many around the world to consider (or reconsider) who and what is important.

The pandemic and climate change have totally different focuses, but both lead to the same outcome: to move occupants of this planet to ask big questions about our existence. To awaken. To change and do better – physically, mentally, emotionally and spiritually.

I've often said that at an individual level our guidance can come as gentle whispers, which, if ignored, will soon become a smack about the head. The same is true of collective guidance. And earth ain't whispering anymore.

Pandemic pandemonium

Q *What was or is the lesson in COVID-19? Why has this pandemic occurred right now, in the middle of so much change? While most of the world was in lockdown, or at least in the early lockdown in Australia, we heard reports that our environment was taking a breather, that people were rushing out to buy seeds for their home gardens, that suddenly people were considering homeschooling as a viable long-term solution for their families. Beyond the health and economic implications of this crisis, what (if any) are the bigger spiritual reasons or lessons for this moment in our world's history?*

A Perhaps the question we really need to ask is: 'How else might our world have reset itself?'

When discussing an individual awakening (as I did in my first book), I highlight the importance of creating stillness, space and silence. In that quiet we can truly see, hear and feel all that isn't noticed when we're busy rushing around and numbing out. The lockdown and isolation of the COVID-19 pandemic created a mass-scale stillness, space and silence for the collective – an important step in any awakening, now just on a global scale.

That stillness, space and silence, such a shocking pause, was the only way, perhaps, for us to take such a moment. Questions generated from that pause were questions that hadn't been so urgently articulated or pursued before. We questioned the very nature of our existence, why we do the things we do and why we do them in the way we've been doing them. Suddenly, stark contrast highlighted the inequalities many had been able to ignore.

Moving through a collective awakening then may follow a similar trajectory to how I've charted a personal awakening. A huge internal transformation must ensue. Cue social and systemic change. This is akin to the collective applying the Mirror Technique I share on page 257. This concept suggests what we witness in others (or the world around us) can be used as a gateway inside ourselves to question where we may hold certain beliefs – and if it's time to shift them. A huge pandemic-shaped mirror has been held up to the world. We've needed to take a long, hard look at ourselves and to decide if this is how we wish to go on.

Following the awakening journey, we can expect that this catalyst will eventually create a vision for a shared future. We need to clear, heal and restore ourselves as a people, and then to become very clear on the world we wish to create and manifest next. I call this the Guidance Cycle (see page 262), and we're moving through a rather macro, rather mass cycle right now. As a group, in order to manifest that which we desire, we will need to bring ourselves into energetic alignment with exactly what we have said we desire. Said another way: let go of the old energy, focus on the new energy and allow more of that goodness to be drawn to us. En masse.

When I said in my last book that all of life is working to support us, I didn't have a disclaimer for a pandemic. All of life *is* working for us. Even a pandemic.

Structurally sound

Q *I've heard you talk about this change moving through our world requiring us to dismantle existing systems and structures. What exactly does this mean? That we no longer need governance? Or supports for our societies? Wouldn't the demolition of such societal structures wreak havoc? And, if we do manage to tear down these constructs, what comes in to replace them?*

A From an energetic viewpoint, our planet and her people are moving into higher levels of frequency and consciousness. In these levels of consciousness, much of what existed on the lower levels cannot survive, including many of the systems and structures we've used to construct our world to date.

Consider for a moment how I explain the realm of the non-physical. Throughout this book, I've referred to their non-attachment, non-judgement, unconditional love and lack of duality, not to mention their lack of physical bodies. Don't worry, we're not losing our physical bodies any time soon! Instead, we are moving closer to a similar vibration – where competition must give way to collaboration, where manipulative power and control must give way to more free and balanced relationships, and where imbalance and inequality must give way to unconditional love of all beings.

Such a utopia is indeed possible. Is it the next immediate step? Probably not. But, when we can see the bigger picture, I believe it can help us better prepare.

So, to the point of our systems and structures. When I've passed on messages, particularly from the High Council of Sages, regarding our systems and structures, they are generally referring to larger societal structures – patriarchy, racism, capitalism – as well as the more micro structures and constraints of our societies – wage inequality, the mental load of women, even the simple disparity between school hours and the standard working day. So many of our world's mechanics are outdated and outmoded, holding people down. This is not higher frequency and cannot be sustained.

What we must remember here is timing – and, more specifically, a *divine* timing. Utopia wasn't built in a day. We can't just rip down these structures and throw caution to the wind. And new physical societal structures need to be built upon strong *internal structures*. Yep, you guessed it – our energy. The energetic structures of our people need rewiring, re-gridding. And to do that, every individual needs to understand their part in the energetic circuit. Without reinforced and clean energy structures, none of the new scaffolding will stand up to pressure.

So when I say we are energetically upgrading the planet, this is what I mean. *We* need to energetically upgrade, plug that energy into the earth, then rebuild around it. En masse, we are now raising our vibrations through individual awakening, contributing to a mass awakening, contributing to a mass rewiring of the structures that underpin our existence here. Lower frequencies cannot survive – but they're not going without a fight! And so, in this messy middle, we are seeing existing societal structures weaken. Eventually they will crumble and fall, just as anything that is not an energetic match for where we are going will.

.+ •

QUESTIONS TO ASK YOURSELF

You might like to meditate on the following questions, use them as journalling prompts, invite your own SST to answer you, or turn an oracle card from The Little Sage Oracle Cards in response.

* How can I build my resilience?
* How can I reinforce my *physical* body to fully show up to our world's (and my life's) challenges?
* How can I reinforce my *mental* body to fully show up to our world's (and my life's) challenges?
* How can I reinforce my *emotional* body to fully show up to our world's (and my life's) challenges?
* How can I reinforce my *energetic* body to fully show up to our world's (and my life's) challenges?

If these questions and answers prompt a deeper enquiry, I've compiled a list of additional resources at helenjacobs. co/ask.

.+ •

What's possible?

We've explored some big questions throughout this book and perhaps we've been building to the biggest questions of them all: are we ever going to turn this around? Will we course-correct? Is it possible we can all just get along? Put simply: what's possible for us next?

The simple answer boils down to what we choose. Nothing is definite; it's our choices that influence and impact the outcome. We cannot simply hope for the best and trust this will all take care of itself. Similarly, we cannot simply think we're doomed – if you believe it, it is so.

There is no magical white knight riding in upon a horse to save us. We have to save ourselves.

Spirit's recent messages very much point to the role the individual plays in the collective, as you've seen woven into the plethora of answers already shared in these pages. Each and every one of us has to awaken to the role we play. In doing so, we also awaken to the power we have in our own lives, and the powerful contribution each of us can make to the whole.

An interesting point spirit makes is the role our earth herself plays in our growth and advancement. It's an aspect of our collective healing often overlooked. Our earth is an incredible healer; she knows what she's doing – our job is to *allow* it to happen. And to do that, we need to come back into a deep respect and harmony with her once more. Just as we are learning – remembering – we are not separate from each other, we must again remember we are not separate from our earth.

Psychically peering into the future, I'm not gazing upon a future set in stone. There are multiple possible outcomes here, and multiple possible timelines. Regardless of which ones I've peered into, the vast majority of them point towards a better future and world for our children, and our children's children.

No matter what we wish to manifest for ourselves or for our planet, if we can imagine it, it is possible. And, so, just what is possible?

Doomsday cometh?

Q *WTF is actually happening in our world right now? My boyfriend says life's a bit of a shitshow and we're all just going to hell in a handbasket. Maybe he's right. Maybe I'm just really naive, but I want to believe we could actually turn it around. Are we going to? I'll admit, though, that doing my bit seems so inconsequential. It's the big guys who need to change and it's looking unlikely that they're going to, or not anytime soon. And we don't have time. What's the point of me driving less and recycling when these steps barely even make a dint? How on earth do we convince everyone else to do their part? I don't want to leave a world like this for our children (and should we even bring more children into this mess?). Is it going to end as badly as we've been told?*

A Things sure aren't looking good. But we are the critical determinant in what happens next.

Spirit shows it to me this way: where we place our energy, awareness and attention is important. The intention behind our actions is important. Recycling, but believing it's all for naught, is the equivalent of taking your medicine but believing you're going to die anyway. We need to be able to remove emotion, namely fear, from this equation. Can we observe what is happening and choose our own sovereign power to make change to the collective? Giving in before ever really getting started is akin to placing yourself on the starting blocks and never intending to race.

Earlier, when we explored manifesting (see page 192), I shared that the intention behind our actions is paramount. More people moving from fear to a deep knowing and trust in where we're going will tip the scales. We need to trust we haven't been led here to only be led here. We need to turn on the trust magnet, not the fear magnet. And then we need to make it really freaking huge!

Believing change is possible is important. We don't necessarily need to know *how* that change is possible, just that it is – then steer our energy and actions in that direction. Our energy is our most powerful asset here. Our energy, when met with aligned belief, faith and *action*, truly can move mountains. And so, as each person moves to bring themselves into this kind of inner alignment, it creates a collective alignment.

Sadly, the same is true in the other direction. Should the fear-mongering take hold and gain momentum, then this is the direction the energy moves in. This is the direction that belief, faith and action begin to align to, and a *very* different outcome is possible. We are indeed at a critical tipping point: what will we choose as *real* for us? And can more of us choose something that isn't real *yet*? We have to be willing to believe in something in order to see it – exactly what you might expect a mass awakening to prompt.

Which outcome do you believe is possible? Choose – then align all you can to move in that direction. Believe you will go to hell in a handbasket and you will. And if this is believed en masse, then the masses will indeed go to hell in a handbasket. Herein lies one of the greatest moments in human history: the recognition that our choice is a powerful force. That *we* are a powerful force, far greater than we've ever before perceived. When we believe that to be true, we will finally see it.

Earth's healing

Q *What can each of us do to raise our earth's vibration? How can we contribute to raising the consciousness and bringing healing to our earth and all her people? Is it even possible for our earth to heal, or are we just too far gone?*

+✦.+✦ • •

A Earth is raising her own vibration. We're not here to *save* her. She can – and will – save herself. But we do need to get out of the way to let her do her thing. We need to stop causing harm to begin with. We need to radically shift our thinking and stop centring ourselves. We need to recognise and trust earth's innate wisdom and learn from her, then honour her.

Let's shift our perspective here: our role is as conduits; we can bring through our true individual vibration, plug it into the earth and feed this vibration into earth's energetic field. When we see ourselves as conductors of energy, when we realise that raising our individual vibrations allows us to bring through higher and higher frequencies that can be sent into the earth's field, into the earth's own energetic grid, we can play a part in a wider interconnected web.

This is how we rebuild the energetic structures on our planet (as hinted at on page 235).

As we each individually remember our true nature, our spiritual being and our ability to reach for higher frequencies and integrate them into our bodies, we are doing it not only for ourselves, but for each other *and our earth*. When I say our energetic bodies underpin our emotional, mental and physical bodies, the same is true for our earth. It all starts with energy.

Just as earth has Four Bodies, she also has a soul and a soul blueprint. She is on her own trajectory of energetic upgrade. Just like us, she too must heal all Four Bodies and her soul. Much attention is focused on earth's physical body – say, our environment and climate change. We're witnessing an emotional release as earth rages with fire and cleanses with floods. A pandemic creates a mindful reprieve, for example. Sadly, not as much attention (*yet!*) is given to earth's energetic field, her spiritual nature and her ability to heal, replenish and restore as all of life can. And this lack of attention is our downfall.

We have forgotten we are part of this energetic ecosystem, not commanders of it. We are not separate from our earth. We are from her; we return to her. Our physical form is intrinsically linked to the earth. We drink her. We breathe her. We are nourished from her – and thus what we are doing to our earth we are doing to ourselves. We are not separate from our earth, we are born out of her. We need to give her pause to rejuvenate, to be released from our constant pillaging and destruction – for we are only pillaging and destroying ourselves.

Each of us brings a unique vibration to feed into this energy grid. We do that by honouring the unique soul mission, or purpose, we've been sent here to uphold. Some of us are focused on raising conscious kids. Some of us are protesting in the streets. Some of us are cheerleading and keeping spirits high. Some of us are changing our behaviours. Some of us are donating money to charity and causes. We are each contributing in our own ways, raising our own vibrations and feeding them into the earth in turn. And we must each be very careful to not assume, or judge, what someone else is or isn't doing.

Our earth knows how to heal. She is healing. She always has been. And as we are not separate from her, our healing is her healing.

Utopian vision

Q *I'd love to know what spirit sees for the future of earth and humankind. No biggie! Please tell me there is something better ahead for us.*

+⁺.⁺˙ .

A As with any of my predictions, what I see isn't set in stone – it's a snippet of possibility we can choose to honour, or make changes to move in a different direction. And, just with any other prediction, the timing is up to the interactivity of all the moving pieces. How long will it take? Well, how long will it take us to act?

Multiple possible timelines are available. Each and every choice we make as individuals has a bearing and impact on not only our individual lives, but also the collective – and therefore on the potential outcomes. This isn't some exact science.

Disclaimers aside, here's what spirit shows me.

Utopia.

Read that again.

No, I'm not kidding. It's possible. Is it coming tomorrow? Don't bet on it.

As our vibrations increase and lower consciousness can no longer survive, heavier and denser vibrations and frequencies won't withstand this future; thus, the outcome is a utopian world of balance and harmony. We're forging ahead to a world no longer reliant on the old structures, systems and beliefs that created it. We are looking ahead to a world where equality and balance are restored. Where feminine wisdom and masculine vision meet and merge, where everyone is seen and valued not only for the role they play, but for who they are.

I've seen snippets of that timeline that include a return to a simpler way of life. A time where we work with energy for medicine. Where we not only get along, but where we recognise, acknowledge and actually celebrate the role we are each here to play. Our currencies change; we return to a kind of bartering agreement – or value currency – rather than a physical fiscal exchange. Our levels of hierarchy and government are more flat and organic. There is no greed and corruption – this is impossible in higher dimensions. All this is possible when all of earth's inhabitants have raised into higher consciousness.

Alas, this takes time.

And I can predict your next question … (psychic joke, did you see it coming?). How long does this take? Your guess is as good as mine.

We can speed up the trajectory and, in truth, I believe this is happening now. And spirit reminds us that, from their perspective, it's all progress.

It would be remiss of me to ignore that one of the multiple possibilities is indeed the earth following a far worse trajectory. In this outcome, things don't bode well for humankind. However, the earth herself is forever expanding and forever rejuvenating, with or without humans. Over many, many years, it would be possible for her to regenerate, even if we did not. When I explore this concept further though, it feels to me like humans would end up somewhere else – we can't have accumulated all this collective karma to just hit a dead end. We'd need to go to some other realm, some other time and space, to complete what was set forth here.

Does this mean I perceive us moving to Mars, or some galaxy far away? Not in the way our movies depict. It won't be because humans take us there, but because the greater cosmic forces – those soul conventions in the sky – conspire to move life elsewhere. And, honestly, that is just too far beyond the stretch of even my imagination.

Such a collective awakening isn't being done alone. As more and more people awaken to their spiritual nature, they're awakening to their own spirit guides and guiding beings in higher, more far-flung realms. With all this inter-galactic, cosmic support beaming in to enough channels and mediums, we can move through this change. We haven't come this far to only come this far.

Remembering

Q *Will we ever remember?*

A We already are.

This is precisely why we're here. Remembering is the whole damn point of what we're going through. And I have every faith that we will remember – but, clearly, not without a fight. Mass up-levelling of consciousness, upgrading our planet and all her inhabitants' frequencies, is not some walk in the park – especially if you perceive yourself to be under threat in that process. We are reaching critical mass; the tipping point is here.

This isn't just about remembering – it's about what we do once we have remembered.

As the masses awaken, as they remember who they really are and why they are really here, then we have no other option but to move the rest of humankind along with us. Your remembering awakens your neighbour. Their remembering awakens their neighbour, until such time as we have all indeed remembered.

Don't forget, earth has her own soul blueprint. Your remembering is just one small part in it! There is an even greater plan than your remembering – but you won't know what that day holds for you until all the family is awake. Only then can you set out to truly enjoy it.

. ✦ •

QUESTIONS TO ASK YOURSELF

You might like to meditate on the following questions, use them as journalling prompts, invite your own SST to answer you, or turn an oracle card from The Little Sage Oracle Cards in response.

* What world do I imagine for myself?
* What world do I imagine for the next generations?
* How do I contribute to that vision?

If these questions and answers prompt a deeper enquiry, I've compiled a list of additional resources at helenjacobs. co/ask.

. ✦ •

Last words

Before we call time on this round of Q&A, Chris would like to turn the tables. For the plethora of questions asked of him over the years, friends, there is only one he's ever really asked in return.

What do you really want?

For all our projecting, anticipation and worry for a potential future that may or may not occur (remember, it's not pre-determined), this one question has the ability to cut through the muck and remind us of our own sovereign power. Honing in on what we really want, tuning into the desires of our soul, we not only reclaim our inherent power to create the future we want for ourselves, we can actually begin to imagine something for ourselves that our minds alone could not fathom – but soul already knows.

Journeying through our own individual awakenings and into a more collective consciousness, the same question applies. As I hope you may have observed moving through these pages, the journey from individual to collective awakening also brings with it an arc in the questions asked. Continue asking questions bigger than ourselves! But before you rush to ask another friend for the answers, ask yourself Chris's question first. *What do you really want?* What do *we* really want for our world, for our children, for our future? Take the time to truly find your answer, then let that be your guiding light. Everything else becomes secondary.

As lovely as it's been over the past decade to have asked so many questions for so many friends, I've often felt conflicted. You see, as much as I've enjoyed this process of Q&A (and deeply appreciated each and every person who has sought me out), I honestly believe it's far more beneficial – and far more prudent in the grand scheme of our greater awakening – for each person to learn to find the answers for themselves. My real work in the world, my soul's purpose, is not to be asking for a friend, but to teach my friend how to ask for themselves.

In an age where we are accustomed to Google immediately spewing forth millions of answers to our most curious questions, we've lost the ability to sit still long enough to seek answers to life's harder questions. Big questions, like the ones we've explored here together, deserve our time and respect. Questions about the very nature of our existence cannot be reduced to a definitive, succinct, sound-bite response, just as they can't be reduced to a brief exploration in a book such as this.

My goal in writing this book, and sharing a smattering of sample questions and answers, is to initiate thought, to catalyse change and, dare I say it, to restore hope in our world – and in ourselves. Perhaps it's naive of me to think that this book won't produce more questions. Such questions, and spirit's answers, have typically elicited such a response for me. Pondering one question only leads to half a dozen more, and so on it goes. If you haven't done so already, be sure to visit helenjacobs.co/ask to download the bundle of additional resources and exercises I've compiled to support your burgeoning game of Q&A. Such a line of enquiry can be fun, a game full of riches if you are willing to enquire a little deeper, and possibly wait a little longer than a Google algorithm to receive your own answers.

My conundrum, then, is that a book such as this is meant to be my last hoorah, a retirement from Q&As. It's becoming more and more difficult for me to keep taking such questions for the growing number of friends wanting to ask them. However, I am committed to helping you ask – and answer – your own questions. This is my true soul work in life. If you are interested in learning how to answer such questions for yourself, I invite you to first explore my book *You Already Know*, and then come on over to my website to find my events, support tools and programs. I have a decade's worth of materials to get you started.

No matter how many similar books may be published, or how many psychics or mediums are in the world (and potentially in cahoots!), the most powerful person holding the answers is *you*. Such psychic and medium abilities reside inside each and every one of us. It's how the Great Mother programmed us.

For now, my friend, it's time to start asking questions for yourself. Don't ask for a friend, be your own friend. Life will always answer, if you let it.

Resources

The Mirror Technique

Your feelings are a mirror. Your jobs, relationships and money are all mirrors. Your Four Bodies – more mirrors. They all highlight the core of who you are, and point to where you can clear, heal or restore to come back into alignment with your true self.

Using outer world events and situations as mirrors, you might see that feeling stuck in your job might mirror a 'stuckness' inside. Hurting in your relationships mirrors hurt in your relationship with self. When money (or anything in your outer world for that matter) doesn't flow, it shows where your inner world isn't flowing. And your own life force, or energy, supports it all. Here, we begin to apply our symbolism anew, looking at all of life in new ways.

Follow these four steps for the Mirror Technique:

- **Identify.** Delve deep to identify what's triggering or challenging you. What's the real problem here? Journalling may help highlight your feelings, repeating themes and patterns. What comes up for you? How do you currently see your world? Home in on the core issue.

- **Reflect.** How you see your outer world hints at the beliefs, emotions or energy within (or about) yourself. Your emotions and feelings highlight what's off-kilter physically, mentally, emotionally or spiritually. The mirror will point to one of your Four Bodies, before taking you in deeper. Your SST or your physical support team of healers and teachers may also support this process.

- **Toolkit.** Once you know your inner landscape, you can determine the supports required to heal. I provide a thorough toolkit in *You Already Know* to help you, as well as support clients to determine their own toolkits via my programs and online communities.

- **Act.** There's no point knowing you can process old pains and hurts, but never actually tending to them.

Some pains are so ingrained we don't know they're there. Others we simply never want to poke at again; there's a reason we've buried them. You don't have to do it alone – and it may just be that the tool you choose to work with includes turning to qualified practitioners to support you where needed.

Go on the bear hunt, and go through whatever is waiting for you.

The Four Bodies

1. Physical

This body is actually composed of another four layers, which I call the 4Ps. We store (and often exchange) energy in each of these 4Ps, so knowing how to clear and balance this energy is vital. They are:

- **Physical.** This refers to the anatomical body, influenced by things such as diet, sleep and exercise. Its physical ailments and disease can highlight what's happening internally when viewed through a more symbolic lens. Movement, food and rest influence the flow of energy through our anatomical body.

- **People.** We each have an energy field. As we physically interact with others, so do our energy fields. Without awareness, we're unconsciously exchanging and absorbing other people's energy fields. Use psychic protection such as white light or crystals like clear quartz, or work with my Ground, Clear and Protect Your Energy meditation on my website.

- **Places.** Consider the energy of buildings, cities, countries and so on. For example, imagine the energetic implications of living in a haunted house, or desecrating sacred lands. Energetically clearing spaces can involve music, sound, crystals, salt water and intention.

- **Possessions.** Energy is transferred into our jewellery, clothing and furniture, and inanimate objects can emanate energy, too. Clearing out unwanted items can help, or cleaning them with salt water and essential oils (determined by what the objects can withstand).

2. Mental

This body refers to witnessing your thinking as an observer. Non-attachment to your thoughts highlights your inner critic. This is one reason why meditation is so important. This body also refers to the stories and limiting beliefs we tell ourselves about ourselves. Use the Mirror Technique (see page 257), therapy and journalling to help with this body.

3. Emotional

There are no 'good' or 'bad' emotions; they are just indicators. Good-feeling emotions can show you where you're in alignment with your own divine life path and soul, while negative-feeling emotions signal the opposite. Allow yourself to feel your emotions and enquire as to what they mean for you.

4. Spiritual or energetic

This is not your physical energy nor stamina but your life force. Working with your chakras is an excellent place to start in understanding the flow of life force energy through your energetic body.

The Guidance Cycle

Following our inner and higher guidance to lead us through an inner transformation will track a predictable pattern I call the Guidance Cycle. This cycle consists of four phases:

- **Clearing.** First, we remove all the debris and gunk from our physical, mental, emotional and energetic layers.

- **Healing.** Next, we repair each of the Four Bodies in the wake of the clearing.

- **Restoring.** Here we take a pause, a moment to recover and recharge before the real action begins in the next phase.

- **Manifesting.** Finally, we are guided into the soul-aligned action steps to take along the next phase of our soul's path.

Working with your SST and intuition, you'll receive specific steps to take, which are clues as to what phase of the Guidance Cycle you're in, as highlighted in the following table. You can also intuitively review the table and notice what phase you're actively working on, and which body you're focusing on, along with suggestions for support and actions to take.

Supports during the Guidance Cycle

	CLEARING	HEALING
PHYSICAL	Detoxing diet and body Letting go/ending/ completing (jobs, relationships, friendships, etc.) Culling (furniture, files, clothing, cupboards, etc.) Moving, renovating, redecorating, relocating	Rest, recovery, stillness, gentle activity Practitioner support (doctors, natural therapies, etc.) Relationship counselling
MENTAL	Reset mindsets, beliefs, attachments, stories Journalling, self-reflection, meditation	Reframing and re-creating beliefs and perceptions Writing new stories and life scripts
EMOTIONAL	Emotional embodiment (sit in discomfort with all feelings until the sensations pass) Self-expression Physical release (writing, boxing class, dancing, etc.)	Forgiveness Acceptance Self-love Unconditional love Compassion
SPIRITUAL/ENERGETIC (FOCUS ON CHAKRAS)	Individual chakra clearing (white light, red light, crystals, sound, reiki, kinesiology) Cutting energy/psychic cords	Balance chakras with one another (white light, crystals, sound, reiki, kinesiology) Protecting boundaries

	RESTORING	**MANIFESTING**
PHYSICAL	Improving diet, sleep and exercise, increasing nutrients New relationships, supports, jobs, homes, etc. Repairing/buying new items Re-energising your spaces	Beginning/creating anew People/supports Establishing a new routine, diet, etc. Receiving new opportunities
MENTAL	Positive affirmations Meditation White space	Living from new perspectives as your new normal See the new beliefs in the outer world
EMOTIONAL	Receiving Opening Loving Giving	Balance shifts to more positive emotions as the baseline
SPIRITUAL/ENERGETIC (FOCUS ON CHAKRAS)	Grounding and protecting energy Flooding chakras with white and red light, transmitting surplus	Balanced and vital chakras Free-flowing energy (life force) in inner and outer world 'In the flow' Outer world matches inner world

Chakras

Chakras are energy centres located throughout the body and its surrounding energy field. Use this table to learn more about the location, symbolism and energetic connections of the seven main chakras.

Seven main chakras

CHAKRA	LOCATION	COLOUR	REPRESENTS
BASE CHAKRA	First chakra at base of the spine	Red	Basic survival and belonging. Material, physical world. Security: physical, financial, career, etc. Sense of grounding and connection to earth.
SACRAL CHAKRA	Second chakra, between the navel and base of the spine	Orange	Inter-relational. Emotions, power and sex. Cravings for physical pleasures, addictions, obsessions. Control and manipulation. Creativity. Feminine energy.
SOLAR PLEXUS CHAKRA	Third chakra, behind the navel	Yellow	Self-image, esteem, power and worth. Confidence. Inner strength.

CHAKRA	LOCATION	COLOUR	REPRESENTS
HEART CHAKRA	Fourth chakra, in the centre of the chest	Green	First of the more spiritual chakras. Love, giving and receiving, emotional processing, attachments, forgiveness and compassion.
THROAT CHAKRA	Fifth chakra, in the neck	Blue	Speaking your truth, expressing, asking. Choice and commitment. Transmitting.
THIRD EYE CHAKRA	Sixth chakra, between the eyebrows/ between the eyes	Purple	Clear seeing; past, present and future; seeing within and outward. Spirit and spirituality.
CROWN CHAKRA	Seventh chakra, at the top of the head	White or golden	Clear knowing; connection to the divine or collective mind. Also affected by thoughts on God, religion or spirituality, divine guidance and trust.

Acknowledgements

A book such as this would never exist without all the friends who've asked their questions, and indeed without Chris and the Council (it's sticking) to reply. I'm so very grateful I've been in the privileged position of asking for a friend, a thousand times over.

I'd like to thank my publisher, Kelly, for asking me to write this book to begin with, and the entire Murdoch Books family for your care in editing, designing, marketing and sharing this book with the world. Book doulas, I thank you.

My family once again read an early version of this manuscript and helped massage it into its final form. Thank you – and for the countless hours of big questions and channelled conversations since Chris showed up in our world. Your questions alone would keep me going.

And to the man who asked me life's best question and to the children whose questions never stop, I love and adore you. Thank you, Gary, Isla and Rose, for embarking on another book-writing endeavour with me (and for all the cups of tea).

We hope you enjoy this book. Please return or renew it by the due date.

You can renew it at www.norfolk.gov.uk/libraries or by using our free library app.

Otherwise you can phone 0344 800 8020 - please have your library card and PIN ready.

You can sign up for email reminders too.

NORFOLK ITEM

30129 086 053 551

NORFOLK COUNTY COUNCIL
LIBRARY AND INFORMATION SERVICE